C0-AYG-767

THE
DISCARDED
WINNIPEG 2 MAN.
CANADA

November, 1963

Dear Carol,

The South, that is, Jackson, Mississippi, is not unassailable.

This is not a civilized society. It is a complex of things borrowed from Christianity, "American ideals," and democracy—distorted and misunderstood. Things are used and sought out in order that the Southern "way of life" can more conveniently continue.

That it has existed and continues to exist with so many inherent contradictions is incredible—and oddly, an indication of man's indomitability, but by no means a credit to the human race and its intelligence.

The South is pathetic.

I think the basic ugly cause here is the absence of cultural exposure and thought.

I'm going to attempt to begin a theater here. I will try to write some sort of perspective. Give me some ideas, cause I don't know quite where to start.

Gil

JOY

I Guess
You Know Already
How Hot It Is Here.
Well, at the Risk of
Being Redundant***
It's Hot as Hell
    Down
    Here
I Feel as if I'm
Neglecting FST
Business—What Little
I Can Do—When I
Hear That You Are
Working So Hard.
All These Little
Pieces of Our Souls
In This Thing . . .
Here Are Letters for
Your Files . . .

Denise

To the
Hearts
and
Hands
of the
People of
Mississippi
and of
the
South
who
Will
make
Democracy
a
Reality

The Free Southern Theater by The Free Southern Theater

A documentary of the South's radical black theater, with journals, letters, poetry, essays and a play written by those who built it

Edited by Thomas C. Dent, Richard Schechner
and Gilbert Moses

The Bobbs-Merrill Company/Indianapolis and New York

The Free Southern Theater wishes to express its gratitude to Mr. Stuart W. Little and *The New York Times,* and to Miss Elizabeth Sutherland and *The Nation* magazine for permitting us to include their pieces about us in this book. We are extremely grateful, as well, to Mr. Dennis Cipnic, Mr. Ray Rohrbaugh, Mr. Bob Fletcher, Mr. Richard Pipes, Mr. Tom Wakayama, Mr. Matt Herron and Magnum Photos for allowing us to use the photographs which appear throughout.

The Bobbs-Merrill Company, Inc.
A Subsidiary of Howard W. Sams & Co., Inc., Publishers
Indianapolis • Kansas City • New York

Library of Congress catalogue card number 68–29294
Manufactured in the United States of America
First printing 1969

There is a certain agony . . .

in going back
while rage grows in you
like an unborn child

or looking out
past history's false mirrors
holding desire in
to smash the glass
dividing the black rain
and you

past spiked fences
spearing my mother's
yellow body skyward

past the ghettoed wharfs
where Amos and Andy
in fish nets
still dance

where my father's bones
freckled bones
gleam in a flute cold sun

past the pyramid
of water worn corpses
of jumped overboard captives

past the green brush
the scarred faces
of Timbuctoo

to the streets
bearing and kissing the howling hot stones

join me in the streets

(Now read the poem backwards)

Gilbert Moses

Driving down slinky New Orleans
Turns me on
And makes me sad.
Out in Desire
Where the Jazz City funk floats
Over the street holes
And grooves above the ditches
That stifle black domestics
And greasy high-conked cats
Screaming
Jumping up and down in their own sweat.
It turns me on
And makes me sad.
Out in Desire
All beauty in chains
Rumbling deep somewhere-between-the-stomach-and-the-brain.
Oh the day will come
Out in Desire
The day will come.

Roscoe Orman

The Free Southern Theater
by The Free Southern Theater

Preface

This book is not about a finished theater. The FST is not finished—washed up; nor is it finished—a fully realized project. The FST has suffered its beginnings, made its mistakes, had its triumphs, gone through many changes. And it is all unfinished, all incomplete. The theater continues. Even as this book is published a new season will have begun; the company will be preparing for its 1969 summer tour.

In this country there is little room for imagination and patience, and there is good cause for impatience. But art—even an engaged, ongoing art—is process. Process is not pacific, nor is it quiet. It can be turbulent, militant, absolutely engaged. But the process still takes time. The proof of art is not in the pudding but in the putting together. The FST has been putting itself together from the beginning, and it continues to put itself together now.

This is a book about many starts, many ideas, many individuals. We were all joined in a single project—freedom. We tried, and some of us are still trying, to make an art about freedom, a freedom through art.

In the spring of 1968 Tom Dent met Lawrence Guyot, leader of the Mississippi Freedom Democratic party. During a long discussion about race and politics in Mississippi Guyot asked, "Is it absolutely essential that the Free Southern Theater exist, or is that a moot question?" Dent answered that if the FST had not existed someone sometime would have created it. Black people must have their own theater. Broadway and regional theater are irrelevant to black lives. There must be a form in which the theatricality of the black church, the black freedom movement, black music, black militancy—black power in its widest and deepest sense—can be made into myth, allegory, public performance. Why not now? Why not see the FST through?

We have tried to shape the book around this necessity, this inevitability. To show how programs have become real despite lack of funds, lack of experience, discouraging advice from the start. Guyot's question also throws light on the real reason the FST has survived as a black theater and not as an "integrated" theater. Indeed it is interesting to think about why the FST has survived at all, after so many people—even people who helped found the theater—have pronounced it dead. The answer is that the FST is not a self-serving project. The *need* for the theater has forced even selfish people to keep it alive.

What precisely is this need? It relates to the need to articulate an experience. There is something in the human spirit that is reflective, that asks for someone to "tell it like it is." The FST came into being to tell it like it is. We have not always succeeded. But that goal is the essence of our dream.

It is not simply that the artists and poets and actors and directors who have made the FST wish to say something. More importantly, there is an audience which cries to express itself. In this sense the FST has always been, and continues to be, a popular theater. The audience is articulate and active—no one who has seen an FST performance can fail to recognize that the audience is the most important and expressive element in it. If the FST can ever match the beauty and virility of its audience it will be a great theater.

We hope that this book will serve as more than a record of where we have been. We want our experience to help others who wish to try something similar. We have tried to include a variety of material, some of it almost unedited, so that the flavor of our experience could come through undiluted.

In a book of this type it is impossible to mention the many, many people who have worked, and are still working, to make

FST a success. Because of the unique nature of FST, because much of the support and interest have come from New York and outside the South, many of our friends do not know each other; many others have never seen the FST perform and have never been to the South. We would like to acknowledge the help of the following people, typical of many others. In New Orleans: Margaret Hellbach, one of our original board members in New Orleans, a restaurateur; Rhoda Dreyfus, another original member of the board, the wife of a New Orleans architect; Celestine Cook, wife of a New Orleans insurance executive; Oretha Haley, a former national board member of CORE; Lolis Elie and his legal firm Collins, Douglas and Elie. These people in particular have contributed to our effort locally, and we have been guests in their homes many times. In New York the FST has been supported through the efforts of the Friends of the Free Southern Theater, a group which has borne the lion's share of the fund-raising burden: Carol Feinman, Joy Manhoff, Ben Pick, and Brooke Aronson. Jean Swinney, June Eastmond Gikouri, Martin Koenig, Joe Midell, and David Rothenberg, press agent and publicist, have been the heart and legs of FST's New York operation.

A special note of appreciation is due Mr. and Mrs. Brock Peters, the current co-chairmen of the Friends of the FST and long-time supporters of the theater, and Allen Mandel and Jules Irving, of the Repertory Theater of Lincoln Center, for through their efforts new means are becoming available. The theater is also fortunate to have the services of a most competent and committed staff in its New York office, Associate Producer Mrs. Roberta Jones, and Miss Jeanne Breaker. We are indebted to a host of entertainers and theater people. Those deserving special mention for their repeated response to emergency calls include Max Roach, Abby Lincoln, Ruby Dee, Leon Bibb, Harry Belafonte, Ossie Davis, Diana Sands, George Tabori, Viveca Lindfors, Madeline Sherwood, Paul Newman, Sidney Poitier, Rod Steiger, Frederick O'Neal, and John O. Killens.

So many people have been instrumental in the development and continuation of the FST. Not all of them are represented in the book. We feel that the FST is their dream as well as the dream of those who are included here. And we wish to say to all the people who have helped: our determination continues; the efforts of all—those mentioned and those nameless—will not have been wasted.

Thomas C. Dent
Richard Schechner
John O'Neal
Gilbert Moses

New York City
1968

1

along speeding highways
southern stars churn/quiet white light
graves unincorporated
                                        is the only insurance

here
        i would study
        the origin of the sisters
find
the genius of american dance
                sitting on the lips
                of a toothless shack

2

below
        many many little pickaninnies cry
drooning like oriental wisemen/
        koolaid
                eases the pain
the music of the race
will suffice
the sleepy hamlets

David Henderson

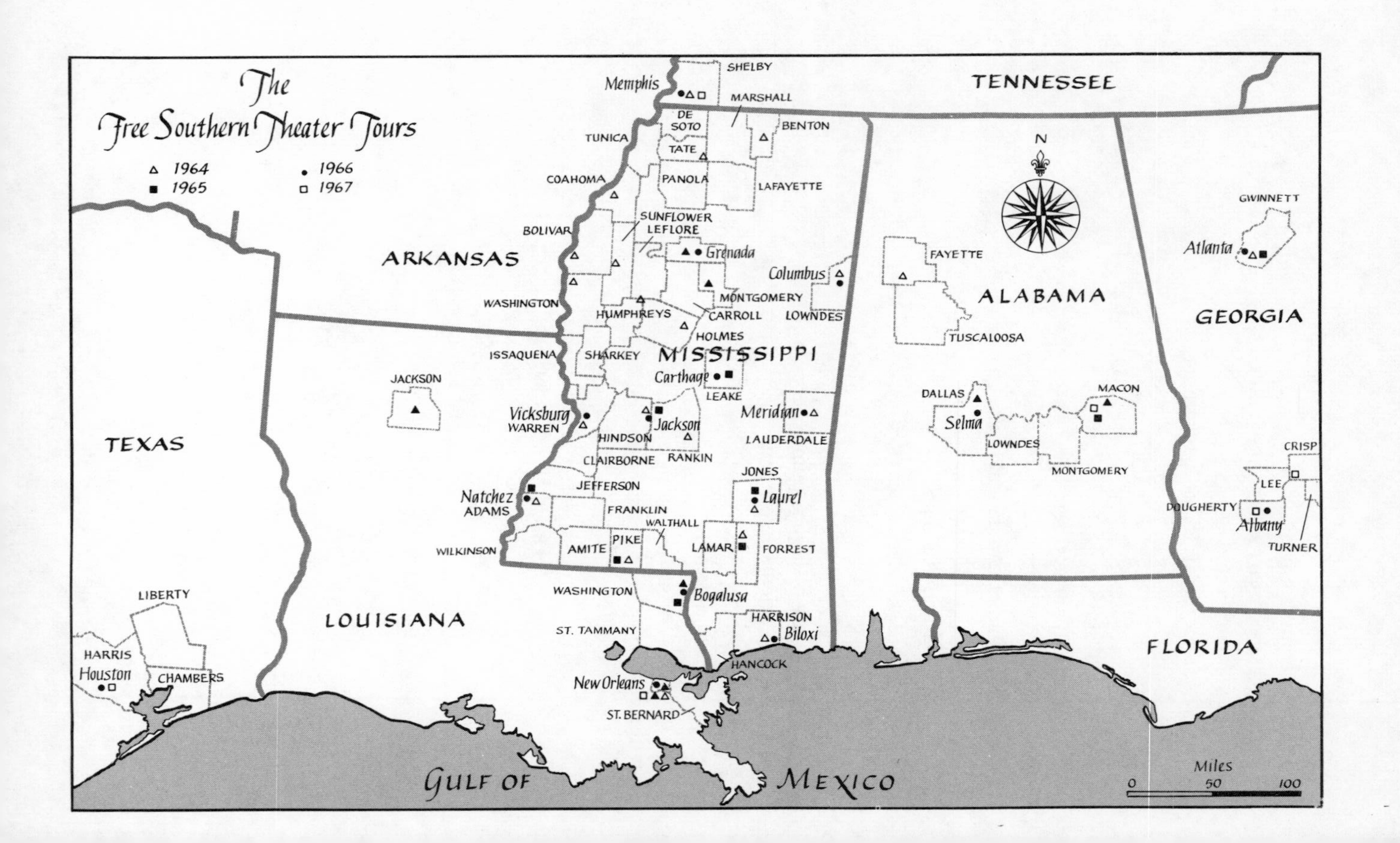
The Free Southern Theater Tours
△ 1964
■ 1965
• 1966
□ 1967
TENNESSEE
ARKANSAS
MISSISSIPPI
ALABAMA
GEORGIA
TEXAS
LOUISIANA
FLORIDA
GULF OF MEXICO
N
Miles
0
50
100
Memphis
SHELBY
MARSHALL
DE SOTO
TUNICA
TATE
BENTON
PANOLA
LAFAYETTE
COAHOMA
SUNFLOWER
LEFLORE
BOLIVAR
Grenada
Columbus
MONTGOMERY
WASHINGTON
HUMPHREYS
CARROLL
LOWNDES
HOLMES
ISSAQUENA
SHARKEY
Carthage
LEAKE
JACKSON
Vicksburg
WARREN
Jackson
Meridian
HINDSON
LAUDERDALE
CLAIRBORNE
RANKIN
JONES
JEFFERSON
Laurel
Natchez
ADAMS
FRANKLIN
WALTHALL
PIKE
AMITE
LAMAR
FORREST
WILKINSON
WASHINGTON
Bogalusa
HARRISON
Biloxi
ST. TAMMANY
HANCOCK
New Orleans
ST. BERNARD
LIBERTY
HARRIS
Houston
CHAMBERS
FAYETTE
TUSCALOOSA
DALLAS
Selma
LOWNDES
MACON
MONTGOMERY
GWINNETT
Atlanta
CRISP
LEE
DOUGHERTY
Albany
TURNER

Part One
THE BEGINNING

GM *Doris Derby, John O'Neal and I met in the winter of 1963 in Jackson, Mississippi, where they were field directors for SNCC and I was writing for the* Mississippi Free Press. *All of us were black, all of us had been involved in theater before we came to Jackson. After we met, and first talked about the need for theater, we got to where we felt we could put down a good case for a Free Southern Theater.*

We decided that Doris, an artist, would concentrate on scenic design; John, who'd just finished his studies at Southern Illinois University, would handle the production and organization; and I would direct and train the actors. We also wanted to sponsor benefits in Jackson, and ask black stars and performers to appear. We wanted to open Jackson up, to bring people there who normally were outside of state control and police authority. We wanted freedom: for thought, and involvement, and the celebration of our own culture.

A General Prospectus for the Establishment of a Free Southern Theater

We propose to establish a legitimate theater in the deep South with its base in Jackson, Mississippi.

Our fundamental objective is to stimulate creative and reflective thought among Negroes in Mississippi and other Southern states by the establishment of a legitimate theater, thereby providing the opportunity for involvement in the theater and the associated art forms.

We theorize that within the Southern situation a theatrical

form and style can be developed that is as unique to the Negro people as the origin of blues and jazz.

A combination of art and social awareness can evolve into plays written for a Negro audience, which relate to the problems within the Negro himself, and within the Negro community.

Through theater, we think to open a new area of protest. One that permits the development of playwrights and actors, one that permits the growth and self-knowledge of a Negro audience, one that supplements the present struggle for freedom.

The above listed objectives are set in accordance with the following observations:

Mississippi—The Caste System in a Cultural Desert

1. *The development of patterns of reflective and creative thought have been restricted.*

a) *Education:* The segregated Mississippi Pubic School system restricts the learning process rather than nourishes it. School textbooks are controlled, discussion of controversial topics is forbidden, teachers have no choice in school programming and are under constant supervision and pressure. It is apparent that competent teachers and honest education will not be the concern of a school system fundamentally built to keep Negroes out of white schools.

Since the majority of the schoolteachers are products of the same system, the students' legacy is inadequate training and an unclear understanding of the world in which they live.

b) *Mass Media:* The newspapers in Mississippi are not a source of information concerning the activities of the community or of the state. The distortions of these newspapers are twofold: (1) What is not printed—any valid information about Mississippi's economics and politics; (2) what is printed—highly distorted and biased articles supporting the Mississippi "way of life." The two Negro weeklies—excluding the *Mississippi Free Press*—financed, and in one case controlled, by the same association which owns the white newspapers, fail to convey true information to the Negro community and are virtually useless and retrogressive in purpose.

i. Television: Controlled and almost never admits controversial topics.

ii. Radio: Jackson, Mississippi, has one Negro radio station which is dedicated to rock-and-roll.

Conclusion: The civil rights movement has greatly affected the vacuum in which the Mississippi Negro lives. Yet, it is still probable that the Negro is the last to be informed of a situation which directly concerns him. *He has been unable to develop naturally because he has found himself in a society which excludes him from its public consciousness, which is, by necessity, his own public consciousness.*

c) *The Negro Community and Its Cultural Resources:* Although Jackson is the largest urban area in Mississippi with a population of approximately 200,000, its 75,000 Negroes are without cultural resources other than one recreation center controlled by the state, one movie theater, two inadequate Y's each with 1,000 members, quite a few juke joints, and about 175 churches. The municipal auditorium is closed to Negroes.

In general, the cultural institutions in Jackson are engaged in a tense struggle for which there exists no immediate solution. Working within a controlled situation, they attempt solutions to problems within the Negro community, but are unable to affect the external cause of the problems.

Conclusion: *Mississippi's closed system effectively refuses the Negro knowledge of himself,* and has stunted the mental growth of the majority of Mississippi Negroes.

2. *There exists a wealth of talent that has been denied the opportunity of development and expression.*

3. *It is necessary that an education program coincide with and augment the program of the Freedom Movement.*

4. *There will be opposition from the present power structure to the theater program.*

A FREE SOUTHERN THEATER

While it is true that the theater which we propose would by no means be a solution to the tremendous problems faced by the people who suffer the oppressive system in the South, we feel that the theater will add a necessary dimension to the current civil rights movement through its unique value as a means of education.

To Movement Friends in New York and Atlanta:

We have organized and are having weekly meetings of a theater workshop. Gilbert Moses is the dramatic director of the workshop; Bill Hutchington, professor of Speech and English at Tougaloo College, is the technical director; Doris Derby and myself are operating in the area of public relations and general flunkies. Doris will help coordinate the concert series.

At the present time we are meeting and working in the Tougaloo College Playhouse. The group is primarily composed of students from Tougaloo and Jackson State Colleges. We are hoping to involve more and more people as time goes by who are not the sole property of the academic community. Our attendance has averaged 25 people, all of whom are responding enthusiastically. Several show great promise.

If things go as hoped for, the group will be ready for public showing within two or three months and we will be able to operate a modest touring and summer stock company by summer. Several contingencies are involved, however. We're trying to feel out the faculty at Jackson State now to see to what extent they will be able to cooperate with the program.

Hopefully, we'll get the material for a repertory company from this workshop which will be a permanent part of our program from now on. As we get people committed to the theater some means must be found for their support if we are not able to raise enough money to provide for their subsistence.

I am in the process of negotiating with the local representative of S. B. Fuller products whereby we may have a franchise for the door-to-door sale of his products in a given area. In such a manner the group could work and pay for itself and still be in control of our own time.

At the present time we have accumulated a total of three scripts for consideration, aside from stuff that either Gil or myself have done; 2 from Langston Hughes, *Jim Crow Jericho* and *Do You Want to Be Free;* and 1 from Nancy Henderson with whom Gil spent some time in New York: *Lo, the Angels.* None of these seem appropriate for the kind of thing we want to do. We therefore are in need of scripts. All kinds of stuff, especially material from Young Black Cats who heretofore have not had the opportunity to have their plays considered for production. Material from old "established cats" would, of course, be all right. We have been promised material from John Killens, James Baldwin, Ossie Davis, and Ted Shine already. They should all be reminded of our needs in this regard.

So concludes this report kind of thing.

Yours for a Free Southern Theater,
John O'Neal

March 9, 1964

To Carol Feinman

Carol,

Hope to arrive in New York either the 12 or 13 of March, to stay for a week and a half.

Why I am coming:

1) To talk, discuss, make plans for, see about immediate fund-raising.

2) To finalize acquisition of technical equipment.
3) To help gather sponsors
4) Gather new scripts where I may
5) and because there is a free ride leaving out of here at 6 o'clock in the morning.
6) To breathe freely, for a while, for a change.
7) To take a look-see at publicity . . .
8) I am dying, utterly, uncontestably (well, incontestablement)

It will be a very difficult trip. I see a picture of myself prancing around New York, talking about the theater in Mississippi. . . . I feel like a vaudeville barker. Exhorting spectators to pay their dues. Step right up and see the fire next time in Mississippi.

Like the rest of America is about to pay their way to see a bullfight, to see the lions clawing the Christians.

Did you see the SNCC advertisement (on the back of *Progressive* for March)? "It takes more than courage . . . to face the combined forces of the resistant South." The reason that this line returns to mind is due to its sadistic implications. This frank and bleeding statement as if the Federal Government didn't exist . . . as if the South were another country, an underdeveloped country, South Africa, apartheid, the SNCC Mau-maus. More than that—it is a new approach to civil rights—casual, understated, sits you back on your reflective haunches, softens the emotional tone of the movement, the freedom struggle, almost puts it in its properly crude and harsh context: a calculated battle, bloody, the Jews and Hitler, the Italians and Ethiopia, early Americans and the Indians, flesh against flesh, a broken head, "Get on out of here, Nigger, I'm the justice here." Broken teeth, a prison cell, a shotgun in the back.

Step right up. Hear the clanker and strut of tanks, the fattening of army ranks, the strained cries of a black face whipped with chains, as we in Mississippi prepare for war.

Pay your dues and watch.

Gil

John Baby,

. . . Baby I know you are going to make it and that the letter you wrote to me is just one expressing that temporary fright before you unleash de blood hounds of hell and scrounge all available asses in to the barn and explode with the theater. You can do it. You will do it. You must do it. Wail, mother——dear.

Tell Gil to cancel them got-to be-damned plans about going back to school. We learn where it's *at* and if it ain't *at* Jackson, Mississippi, it ain't no-where. All of New York is buzzing. There will be money to carry on. And there will be talent galore, so much so that traffic cops will be needed to direct the Nothingham northerners in and out of the place. You guys stumbled on to the most exciting idea of the Movement in a century. It would be a crime against nature if you strayed away from this promise just to go to school. Please baby . . . please.

Sit down and put your heart and soul into an article telling the folks why the rocks are crying out for a theater of the people and by the people and for the people. Wail, baby!

The Snake will make it there when the real crucial period occurs. Fret not.

Love,
Len* [Holt]

GM *We wanted the theater to deal with black artists and the black audience. But its political aims reflected the political aims of the Movement at that time: integration. One of the first steps of rebelling against the Southern society, then, was to make an effort to integrate anything. A large part of the excitement generated by the idea for the theater was centered around the fact that it would be integration operating in the deep South, and integration operating in the mainly unintegrated American theater. So two generic ideas were in conflict from the beginning:*

* Len Holt, a SNCC lawyer.

The development of a black style of theater (or whatever term we came up with to call what we were doing), and an "integrated" theater, based on pre-existing structures. We sent a copy of our prospectus to Richard Schechner, who was then professor of Drama at Tulane University in New Orleans. Richard's brother Bill had been a roommate of mine at Oberlin.

February 19, 1964

Dear Miss Derby, Mr. Moses, and Mr. O'Neal,

I tried to phone you just before I left for New York, but was unable to reach you—so this letter is a substitute. I have your plans in my hand and have read them over, and I am very impressed. I even discussed them briefly with some friends in the New York theater. I think the idea of bringing live theater, either as a separate program, or as part of the rallies, to Mississippi towns can have a real and important effect on the whole civil rights movement there; the idea is: (1) dignity and pride and (2) social action.

If you can get the people I can arrange to spend a good part of June in Jackson directing a play or two so that you can perform them in Jackson and around Mississippi—any play you choose; my body and talents, so much as I have, are yours. I can't spend the whole summer, I have a book to finish, and work here to do, but June is yours.

Richard Schechner

GM *Richard came to Jackson that June, John and I put him up on a makeshift bed in the corner of our living room, and the three of us settled into a three-day marathon meeting that resulted in Richard's acceptance of our offer to become a third producing director and the making of a new prospectus by the three of us, this one designed to raise money.*

The Free Southern Theater Fund-Raising Brochure

For the first time live, integrated theater is being established in the deep South. The Free Southern Theater of Tougaloo College* this fall begins its initial season with a permanent ensemble company in Jackson, Mississippi. The company will tour rural Mississippi, Alabama, Georgia, and neighboring states, performing for Negro and, when possible, integrated audiences. Later, other Free Southern Theaters will be established in other states.

THE PLAYS: Dramas concerned with the political and moral dilemma of our time, by such authors as James Baldwin, Bertolt Brecht, Ossie Davis, and Langston Hughes, as well as musicals, comedies, classical works, and improvisations.

THE STAGE: Specially equipped halls, churches, barns, fields—wherever there is space and an audience.

THE COMPANIES: Participants from local communities and, with the cooperation of appropriate unions, professional actors, directors, and technicians.

By themselves, protest and political action cannot sufficiently alter the present situation. In the South today, there is an educational and cultural void which must be filled. For this purpose the theater is uniquely equipped.

The Free Southern Theater will act as a stimulus to the critical thought necessary for effective participation in a democratic society.

The Free Southern Theater can:

- promote the growth and self-knowledge of a new Southern audience of Negroes and whites.
- liberate creative talent that has been denied the opportunity of development and expression.

* Tougaloo, an accredited interracial college outside the jurisdiction of the Mississippi State Legislature, provided support to the FST in many vital areas. Because of this support the FST, in its pilot project, called itself the Free Southern Theater of Tougaloo.

• provide a forum in which the Negro playwright can deal honestly with his own experience, express himself in what may prove to be a new idiom, a new genre, a theatrical form and style as unique as blues, jazz, and gospel.

• emphasize the universality of the problems of the Negro people.

• strengthen communication among Southern Negroes.

• add a cultural and educational dimension to the present Southern freedom movement.

• assert that self-knowledge and creativity are the foundations of human dignity.

The Free Southern Theater will run from September through June, presenting five plays the first season. Because of low incomes and community structure in Mississippi, the performances will be free of charge.

The Free Southern Theater will be structurally and administratively independent, with a National Board of Sponsors and a Local Board of Patrons. The National Board will provide artistic consultation and fiscal guidance, encourage the participation of professionals and assist in fund-raising efforts; the local board will be concerned with the needs of its particular theater, enlisting the support and participation of the community.

The Free Southern Theater depends entirely on private donations. Contributions are tax deductible.

The New York Herald Tribune
April 2, 1964
They'll Take Drama into the South
Stuart W. Little

Free Southern Theater has been established on a nation-wide basis to extend the live theater into the deep South, beginning with a pilot project in Jackson, Mississippi.

The theater has the backing of leading Negro and white playwrights, performers and producers, including James Baldwin, Harry Belafonte, Theodore Bikel, Ossie Davis, Ruby Dee, Langston Hughes and Robert Ryan.

The idea originated in Jackson with Gilbert Moses of the Student Nonviolent Coordinating Committee and Richard Schechner, editor of the Tulane Drama Review, among other founders.

Plays that reflect the struggle of the American Negro will be staged. "The audiences will be Negro and, in time, integrated."

The Free Southern Theater has set forth its main objectives and operating methods in a five page pamphlet that endorses live theater as the most effective medium to combat "the degrading effect of inferior education"; the ignorance in which the Negro is kept by "the omissions and distortions of local press, radio and television"; and "the deliberate exclusion of the Negro community from all but the most meager cultural resources."

The pilot will be a ten week season in Jackson beginning June 13. Seven plays are scheduled: "Purlie Victorious" by Ossie Davis, "Do You want to Be Free" by Langston Hughes, "Lower Than the Angels" by John O. Killens; two one act plays, "Day of Absence" and "Happy Ending" by Douglas Turner, "Great Gettin' Up Morning" by Ann Flagg; and a modern adaptation of "Antigone."

A permanent stock and repertory company will be established in Jackson with mobile units to tour surrounding areas. The audiences the company will encounter for the most part will never have seen live drama. Performances will be given in schools, churches or in the open.

Initiated by SNCC, the Jackson project will be handled by the Council of Federated Organizations, which includes major civil rights groups in Louisiana and Mississippi, and will be assisted by Tougaloo College.

Fund raising is being handled in New York. The immediate goal is $100,000. Contributions, scripts and offers of participation are being accepted in care of Philip Rose Productions, 157 West 57th Street.

GM *Richard went off to New York, to do research for a book he was writing and to do some fund raising. Carol Feinman, an old friend with connections all over New York, and Joy Manhoff, wife of the playwright Bill Manhoff, volunteered to head up the first New York Fund-Raising Committee. By this time we had accumulated a dazzling National Board of Sponsors. New York was buzzing, and John and I, in Jackson, found ourselves resplendent with a New York office, a brochure and two prospectuses, patrons, a Jackson office, three producing directors, one actress (Denise Nicholas, who left the University of Michigan and political science behind her to come and work with us and marry me), a group of students . . . and no theater.*

Madeline Sherwood, a New York actress who had come down to volunteer to lead some improvisation classes and walked in to find us typing, fund raising, stewing over whether to move the "theater" to New Orleans as Richard had suggested, organizing files, and writing letters, underlined our thinking. "Do it now, don't wait." We decided we couldn't wait any longer and began work on a production.

July 11, 1964

Dear Richard,

John and I realized that we had never tried to start a theater in Jackson. Anyway, we've been dying of inactivity, atrophic. Some of us (me) have substituted this theater for our own creativity!

So, to assuage this situation, and because it is just a good thing, we're beginning with *In White America* immediately.

We're using a few local actors and one professional, Susan Tabor. Jackie Washington, a young folk singer from Boston with one Vanguard recording to his credit, will play the guitar. I will direct. John O'Neal will act and produce. It will be a simple production and we'll take it to the Freedom Schools and communities.

Gilbert

July 14, 1964

Dear Gil and John

Your letter received. Work must commence. Because you have not run a theater before is no proof that you shouldn't/can't run one now. In fact you have to run it.

You say [in another letter] that final decision on New Orleans will be determined by your tour. We have already made that "final decision." The money-raising proposals and my participation depend upon New Orleans. If that decision is to be changed —and I certainly hope it is not—you must let me know at once. I am not about to make a fool of myself and spend vital energies only to find out that the theater has vanished. I mean—to keep my personal commitments out of this for the moment—I don't want to solicit money in formal proposals which must be written out and speak to the President of Tulane University about a plan that is not agreed on. We decided on the New Orleans move, the money from Rockefeller and Ford is geared that way, etc. Quite frankly, just as you have invested your personal lives in this thing I have invested mine. The contacts in the theater which I have are good for one time only. If the project succeeds these contacts will continue to be helpful. If the project fails for the *wrong reasons*—inefficiency, incompetence—there will be no further help coming from these people. We can't call on Mac Lowry, Kazan, etc. twice. If the theater fails for the right reasons —harassment, lack of community interest—that's a different matter. I see no reason for it to fail for the "right reasons." We can make it go. But we must work. IN WHITE AMERICA IS A

GOOD IDEA IF COUPLED WITH THE LARGER PROJECT IF IT IS TRULY A "PILOT" OF THE FST. To make it part of the larger project it must end its tour in New Orleans and work must begin there on the facility.

Damn it, you had this great idea for a theater—don't let it throw you now, and don't go back to the time-wasting, one show now one show later, amateur idea. Get the grand idea to work. And then we'll all be able to work *in the theater* and to achieve the *Movement goals* we all want to achieve.

Keep in close touch, because lack of communications can be killing. It has already damaged our faith in each other. I have lost faith in you doing what you are in Mississippi to do—namely to lay the groundwork for *the continued and long-range success of the FST*. Your production of *In White America* can dovetail brilliantly into this if you capitalize on its opportunities. You have lost faith in my cooperating with you, believing, I am sure, that I have "taken over" the theater. That can only be true if you allow me to take it over.

If I lose faith in you or if you lose faith in me then there will be no theater. Neither "your" FST nor "my" FST—nothing; there will only be wrecked feelings, misspent money, and frustration. And no one, least of all the people we want to get to, will benefit. These are axioms, they are not debatable.

What must be done now is to repair the gap in our communications, to get to New Orleans with your production, to arrange the facility, to contact the community, to pick our plays for the season, to pick the core of our actors. THEN WE CAN TRULY BEGIN THE THEATER WORK.

Atrophy will only atrophy you more. It is a continuous, contagious disease and must be treated. You're right when you say that work is the cure. But that work must fit into the larger project. And that larger project is a theater that will endure and grow for many years.

I expect to hear from you at once on these things.

Richard

July 19, 1964

Dear Richard,

Your questions and anxieties are well and correctly directed. The main fault is the breakdown in communication—you are unable to know what we're doing—and we are unfamiliar with your activities.

What we are doing now is an extremely important step in the larger idea of the FST for us. It is the realization in part of the original ideas—TO PRESENT PLAYS THIS SUMMER FOR FREEDOM SCHOOLS AND COMMUNITIES. It will allow us to make contacts in the best manner for the future FST tour. Rather than presenting an idea to the people here who are already disillusioned, who distrust new ideas, who are ignorant of the goals of the FST, we have something real to give them, and a promise of an even better example later.

When we come to them in December we will neither be seeing the people nor the stages we must play in for the first time. During this tour we will also search for talent. Who knows what we'll find.

This production will be simple—with a few lights and one platform, hardly one which we will be able to present in N.O. Although we must make publicity contacts in N.O. in re this production, I suggest we confine performance to Mississippi. We also fear the lack of time. For after this production, all attention must be turned towards N.O. and setting up of the year's program.

Only one actor is professional, Susan Tabor, Equity; the rest are college recruits from the Summer Project. These students have their own source of income, so the only expense will be travel. I have already written to Erika [Munk, Managing Editor of *TDR*], and will go to N.O. July 22, 23, 24, to make initial facility contacts.

When you read our proposed touring schedule, you will understand that we are in the process of mobilizing an audience for the FST. The first performance here in Jackson will be to a selected audience only. Three very prominent local Negroes are sending out invitations (donations requested at the performance) and are heading a theater committee in Jackson.

For us, these are the priorities: (1) to mount *In White America,* (2) to familiarize our public with FST, (3) To select facilities in N.O., (4) to choose the plays which will be done (for only then will we be able to select our company—when we have some idea of who we will need), (5) to select the company.

When I say *In White America* is important to us, I mean that O'Neal and I have a commitment to Mississippi. This production not only fulfills this commitment to Miss., and to the people who are interested in and working for the FST in New York, but to ourselves, as initiators of this idea. We have been to a large part paralyzed by the FST's bigness, by its importance, by the fact that under any and all *circumstances it must not fail . . .*

Please, I am not afraid to play the fool. In a sense, to spin such a golden web in New York when nothing has been accomplished in the South is to play the fool. We are tired of our parts. You say people have all along asked, "What are they doing now," and "What will they be doing this summer," and you were dumbfounded—*WELL, NOW YOU HAVE SOMETHING PROUD TO POINT TO!* You may say, "There is a simple pilot project now in Miss.—one which will take stock of our audiences—one which will set up contacts and playing places—one which will insure protection for our official theater, etc. etc.

Never did we consider the FST not a dangerous undertaking. In talking to everyone we have stated that everything will be done to lessen this danger. We are now going to court this danger and *WE NEED YOUR SUPPORT*.

A sense of timing is extremely important. Both John and I feel that the time for a production is *NOW*.

You reiterate that the FST is a great idea. You know that ideas have no dimension and that the people behind them must supply their depth. Then it follows that what must be backed is people. You are at the moment not only backing yourself but *me and John.* There are obvious deficiencies on our end—age, experience, indecisiveness, yet we are determined and committed to this theater.

Your concerns are correct. Continue writing. We feel at this point we are doing a great deal of hard and important work. Besides, we are about to play the most exciting theatrical circuit in America. We will send weekly reports.

Gilbert

1964

In White America
by Martin Duberman

Company

John O'Neal—actor, technical director, producer
Susan Tabor—actress, costumes
Denise Nicholas—actress, office staff
Gilbert Moses—director, actor, producer
Lester Galt—actor, technical director
Eric Weinberger—actor, stage manager
Jackie Washington—music (Roger Johnson substituted for Mr. Washington at the beginning of the tour due to Mr. Washington's illness. Gilbert Moses played the New Orleans performances.)
Cynthia Washington—publicity, technical assistant

Tour Schedule

July 31 —Tougaloo College, Tougaloo, Miss.
August 1 —McComb, Miss.
August 2–4—Hattiesburg, Miss. (2 performances)
August 5 —Biloxi, Miss.
August 6 —Gulfport, Miss.
August 7–8—Meridian, Miss.
(August 7 performance canceled for Chaney, Goodman, and Schwerner memorial service)

August 9 —Jackson, Miss.
August 10 —Canton, Miss.
August 11 —Vicksburg, Miss.
August 13 —Greenwood, Miss.
August 14 —Greenville, Miss.
August 16 —Mileston, Miss.
August 17 —Ruleville, Miss.—matinee
Indianola, Miss.—evening
August 18 —Clarksdale, Miss.
August 19 —Batesville, Miss.
August 21 —LeMoyne College, Memphis, Tenn.
August 25 —Sacred Heart Church, New Orleans, La.

August 1, 1964

Joy,

I'm packing, finishing off letters and, and, and, I did a lousy performance last night . . . maybe because of lack of training and experience . . . I wander all over the damned stage . . .

McComb this evening . . . and if God's willin' and the creek don't rise, we'll continue . . . I don't know whose side that cat's on . . .

Anyway, give my regards to your husband . . . and maybe you'll come to the New Orleans performance? . . . if it comes off . . .

There was a N.Y. Times reporter at the performance last night . . . it's really bad that we can't get any publicity up there for this. The dress rehearsal was alright . . . we did it for COFO people . . . the communal thing . . . it was too much . . . so we all stood and sang Freedom songs for 15 minutes. It was beautiful. Response has been stupendous . . . everyone seems to love it—dig it, etc.

Go now . . . hope to see you soon.

Love,
Denise

GM *Schechner used his influence to get to the large foundations, Rockefeller and Ford, but they refused to fund us. At first, ostensibly because the FST was not incorporated; then, after we became incorporated, they refused to give money through Tougaloo, or Dillard University, both predominantly black colleges; and then, when our structural organization became even more solid, because the FST was "too explosive"; and then, because . . .*

August 3, 1964

Dear Gilbert,

It seems as if the FST is to be a community theater thing for this first year. We just don't have the money for more, nor does it seem as if we will get the money. The foundations will do nothing until we have our own non-profit status. I haven't heard from Ford but Rockefeller told me on the phone that they would not give money. They would not elaborate on the reasons. Tulane is scared to sponsor us, so we must wait on Rockefeller until our non-profit thing comes thru. Even then there is no guarantee, but as Crawford told me, "You don't want to apply now and get turned down. Wait until there is a good chance." I have written to Mac Lowry but have not had an answer from him. We have taken action to have Tougaloo apply for the Norman Fund money. We should get 2 to 5 thousand from them. But even with this money, our total will be under 10 thousand—and therefore we can't pay salaries to anyone but you, John, maybe one other.

So this raises serious questions about the company. We won't get a Louis Gosset or a Severn Darden to stay for a year for no money, or for room and board. And since we aren't charging admission, we can't even promise room and board for the full year. Our touring program is jeopardized as well, because we can't afford cars, etc. We have to use the transportation at hand, which means the cars of the people working with us.

I understand and don't understand what you mean by "overbearing." I don't try to be overbearing, but I guess I am. All I can say is that I'm trying to work as best I can in a project that we all know has, at present, more going for it in ideas than in long-range accomplishments. In order for the long-range accomplishments to add up we will have to work with what we have and make it go—or try to make it go—

1. Local people, who most probably have part-time work elsewhere.

2. A core of our own people who will work for nothing or for subsistence.

3. Local support in terms of some money, some living accommodations (on the road).

4. New plays.

5. Classics.

We can make it go, I think.

Now of all the people I've talked to there is one, Murray Levy, who probably would come down for subsistence. He is a producer and an actor (Chuck Mee, whose opinion I respect, says he is a good actor). He works for Lorraine Hansberry now and thinks the FST is a good thing and will come down for little. And then there is Peter de Rome, who has already given up his job and will come down. I will come down with him and help him set up before returning here.

But how in god's name are we going to hold auditions when we can only say to actors—

1. We can't pay you.
2. We can't pay your way down.
3. We don't know how long the project will survive.

It is at that level that we're working at present. I suggest that you permit me to audition people. My question is, however, can we pay subsistence? Certainly we can for you, John, and Peter. But how many more? At $40 per week for the three of you, that runs to $120 per week, $600 per month, $5,600 for the nine months. That's about ⅔ of what we've raised thus far. If we go to the skeletal budget (which we *haven't* raised), we still can't pay for the kind of actors we want. We're left then with a community theater situation, with the four of us as staff (five if we include Denise). From there we can maybe build—raise more money, etc. But I don't see what we can offer the Gossets of the world who do have their careers, etc.

You tell me, for on this Monday morning I am very depressed and unable to think clearly. My mind is dizzy and I feel hopeless. I know the thing isn't hopeless. But an already depressed state of mind was accelerated by your letter and now things look dim indeed. I await your instructions.

But of course I want us to agree on principles—and although we don't have much choice (money being what it is)—let us agree on them anyway:

1. Community theater structure with as much professional cooperation as we can get and afford.
2. Home-base—New Orleans; touring—Mississippi.
3. New plays, classics (including contemporary classics).

As for the personal problems, I don't know what to do about them. I think we must all continue to work. Perhaps they will then smooth themselves out, or at least submerge themselves in the larger prospect. That is, the work on the theater itself will cause many of these problems to vanish—as will the fact that we will all be together in the fall. When I get responses to the letters I am sending to those who are auditioning I shall let you know. The response will in some sense be a guide to what will come—how much we can expect people to come from here and how much we will have to rely on local talent. The big difficulty of local talent is, of course, touring. The only people who can tour for 3 months are the unemployed or the rich. We won't get many rich and the unemployed need salaries. So what do we do?*

Richard

* In the fall of 1966 the FST received a three-year grant of $62,500 from the Rockefeller Foundation.

The Nation
October 19, 1964
*Theater of the Meaningful**
Elizabeth Sutherland

Jackson, Miss.

"You are the actors," said John O'Neal, one of the founders of the Free Southern Theater, to the largely Negro, largely youthful audience sitting on folding chairs, benches, cots and the ground, behind a small frame house in Ruleville, Miss. They were waiting to see what was, for probably all of them, their first live play. The "stage" was the back porch; there was no curtain, and lights hadn't been necessary because it was mid-afternoon. Down the road, a few feet from the house, came a pickup truck with a policeman at the wheel, and a large German police dog standing stiff and ominous in the back. It drove by once, then passed back again. An elderly Negro began to trim the grass around his house next door with a noisy power mower. "Why does he do that right now?" I asked Roger Johnson, a young Negro from Boston who does the lighting for the company. "He's one of the local Toms," Johnson shrugged. Finally the play began; it was Martin Duberman's *In White America,* less a play than a dramatic reading of Negro history based on historical documents dating back to the slave trade.

Sharp-eyed policemen and "Uncle Toms" came as no surprise to O'Neal, a young Negro actor from Southern Illinois University, and 22-year-old Gil Moses from Cleveland, Ohio, who directed this production. Moses' wife, Denise, plays the role—which includes the powerful Little Rock scene—made famous off-Broadway by Gloria Foster. Both men are staff members of the Student Nonviolent Coordinating Committee. They organized the theater last spring, with Tougaloo College outside Jackson, Miss., as a home base; they have since set up new headquarters in New Orleans (Box 2374), where Richard Schechner,

* The article was written during the Summer '64 tour.

editor of the *Tulane Drama Review,* joined them recently as third producing director. Most of the company previously had only college acting experience, although one member, Eric Weinberger, had worked with the Living Theater, and Gil Moses had done a little off-Broadway work.

Their version of *In White America* was highly professional and compared very favorably to the original. This first production, given in thirteen towns during a three-week tour of Mississippi last August, was not intended as a sample of what the Free Southern Theater intends to do but as an experiment: to find out how Mississippi Negroes, most of whom had never seen a theatrical performance before, would react; and to ascertain what sort of theater should be developed. Author Duberman has pointed out that his work was originally addressed to white liberals—not to Mississippi Negroes. Much of its irony and humor eluded them and they occasionally laughed when they were not supposed to, or vice versa. They clapped equally for Booker T. Washington delivering his conservative "five fingers speech" and for Black Nationalist Marcus Garvey. Members of the audience who started to join in singing with the cast would sometimes be hushed by others more decorous. One performance, in the coastal town of Gulfport, turned into a small disaster because it was held in a movie theater and the audience, expecting at least one chase scene and three corpses, expressed its sense of betrayal with loud complaints and constant interruptions.

Elsewhere, response was noisy in a different way. As the actors made their pleas for justice or denounced the white man's cruelty, old women and young men would shout: "That's right!" "Amen!" "You tell it!" In Ruleville, Mrs. Fannie Lou Hamer watched intently in the audience as Denise Moses delivered a Negro woman's account of being beaten by whites. Mrs. Hamer, who recently made a stirring appearance at the Democratic Convention as a delegate from the new Freedom Democratic Party, is a former plantation worker and was beaten to insensibility last year for voter-registration work. There was no need to tell her "you are the actors."

"We got the best reaction in churches," said O'Neal, and certainly the response to one performance I saw, at the First Union Baptist Church in the large town of Meridian, would have pleased most actors. Meridian has a good number of middle-class Negroes, and their reaction was quiet, respectful, sophisticated. The most interesting "theater," though, was the new and unfinished community center in the tiny town of Mileston. The center has been a labor of love for a remarkable white man from California, who raised $10,000 for the project and built it himself with a young white helper and local Negro aid on occasion. That afternoon, the play was performed with one wall of the building still missing; the stage stretched out into a real cotton field. As night fell the actors relaxed in nearby homes, while Negroes stood guard outside with shotguns and rifles. The reason was easy to find: in front of one of the homes stood the charred automobile of a Negro civil rights worker which had been fire bombed by whites only three weeks earlier. Farther down the dirt road, in a frame building just like thousands of others in Mississippi, several members of the cast were eating sandwiches and talking or playing cards. A group in the kitchen argued about Brecht's poetry; in an adjoining bedroom, Roger Johnson was telling what happened when he was arrested in the no man's land called Yazoo City. "I just shuffled and scratched my head, yas*suh*, yas*suh*," he said, doing an Amos and Andy around the bed; "I shuffled and scratched all the way to jail." He was released not long after; a bit of acting knowledge comes in handy around Yazoo.

Local whites came to see the play four times. On one occasion, they were local liberals; another time, members of a Mennonite sect. In Vicksburg, on the Mississippi, two white students who had dared to go to Northern universities instead of Ole Miss were among the audience. "One of them even came to the party we had afterward," said a summer volunteer.

And then, toward the end of the tour, there was the performance at Indianola, a rural town located in Senator James Eastland's Sunflower County and the birthplace of the White Citizens' Council. The Summer Project had established a beachhead at Indianola only recently and the play was to be given in the red brick building of the new Freedom School there. Dark was just falling and I was standing alone on the porch while the lights were being set up inside. Suddenly a stream of white police cars came up the driveway, followed by a long line of lights from other cars; it looked like a very orderly lynching party. Forty-two white-helmeted policemen poured out and a man in sports clothes and straw hat walked up to the porch: "There are twenty-five people here who want to see the play. Can they come in? There won't be any trouble," added the man, who turned out to be the sheriff.

They came, of course, the whites: lawyers and other professionals, small businessmen, a few farmers. No wives or daughters to make it at least look like a friendly visit or social occasion. As for the police, many of them had been deputized for the night: not exactly a reassuring species. While the twenty-five guests sat down together in several rows toward the back, the theater became jammed to the rafters with local Negroes; the temperature must have been at least 110 degrees.

Outside, where it was cooler, the police stood in clusters around the building. One group held a very calm, very hopeless discussion with a young white volunteer. "Do you believe God intended black and white to mix?" he was asked. "You're a student, have you had any courses in genetics?" said another. "Northerners can't understand our problems," came from a third officer. "I'm from Georgia," the student replied.

As the evening progressed, you could see that the cast was playing to the white men with everything they had. Some of the whites were laughing, a few clapped. When the freedom songs which end the play were sung, and the Negro audience joined in, the familiar words seemed to ring out as never before. Neither the rows of white men inside, nor the forty-two badges outside, could diminish the stirring voices of all those black men, women, youths and children.

"Which side are you on?" goes one of the songs, and there was, unfortunately, not too much question about this. I returned to Indianola two days later, at the invitation of the sheriff, to talk with some of the whites who had seen the play about their reactions. There was, the sheriff said when we arrived, only one person available: the County Clerk. That gentleman sat alone in a smallish room which had two entrances, for white and Negro. Quietly, with total hostility, he explained that he had gone to the play to find out what the Summer Project was all about. He thought it was well acted, historically accurate as far as he could judge—and inflammatory. The production confirmed his suspicion that the project was Communist-infiltrated. When asked for specific examples of this in the play, he referred only to its general tone, the point it was driving toward. "The project was supposed to teach citizenship and voter registration. There's nothing in the play about those things. Anyway, there's no problem with voter registration in this county—Negroes can come down any time they want to."

From his tone, there obviously wasn't much point in asking how come less than 2 per cent of the eligible Negroes in his county had been registered, or why the federal government had decided to bring suit against the local registrar. There wasn't much point in our talking, period. Our idea that the whites might have come to the play out of some desire for understanding or communication was neatly punctured—or perhaps those who thought differently from the clerk weren't talking. Of course he was right in one sense: anything which encourages the Negro to stand up for his rights *is* revolutionary in Mississippi.

During the performance of *In White America* at Greenville, a man in the audience came up on the stage as a pre-Civil War scene between a white master and a slave was about to begin. He had obviously believed O'Neal's opening words: "You are the actors." But then he stood there, frozen, until Gil Moses finally whispered to him to leave. Afterward the man explained, "There was so much I wanted to say and I had it all figured out. But when I got up there in all that light, I just couldn't."

Somehow, O'Neal feels, a way must be found to incorporate such people into the action. Moses also believes strongly that in addition to becoming a permanent professional repertory company (they are now working on two new productions), the Free Southern Theater should stay in each town a week or two, build a new play around its history and themes, hold workshops. They are less concerned about the type of plays produced and the ability of the local Negroes to understand unfamiliar material or language. "It's a question of how the material is put across," said O'Neal. "Any play can be used if it is given relevance. We can do Shakespeare—let Hamlet be Senator Stennis' liberal son, to give a wild example. Anything, as long as the audience makes connections."

Let no theater lover conclude, however, that this is a group of mere propagandists. All are concerned with aesthetics, all are aware of the message vs. art debate. "Our audiences were more grateful than critical," said O'Neal. "We want to change that too."

Part Two

PURLIE AND *GODOT*

GM *We had begun.*

Now we had to figure out a way to continue to exist. We needed a black community in the South large enough to support the theater, and even before the first tour we knew we would end up in New Orleans.

Relocation of FST headquarters from Jackson to New Orleans, however, was regarded in the back of our minds as a cop-out. New Orleans has a large middle-class black section which we hoped to tap as backers. Richard Schechner lived in New Orleans and could involve himself fully in FST if New Orleans was chosen as our operating base. We as actors felt we could use the distance from the Movement to concentrate on our art. We went to New Orleans.

Idealistically, however, we felt that we were beginning to separate ourselves from the Movement, and the people to whom we were first committed.

Still, there was a great deal of excitement and a lot of work to be done. A theater building had to be located, living facilities found, a local board formed, actors hired, money raised, the Mississippi tour planned.

Dear Actor,

As fund raising for the Free Southern Theater continues it becomes clear that we will not be able to pay anything more than subsistence salary at the beginning of this year. We are faced with the unique opportunity of playing for audiences who have rarely, if ever, gone to the theater. But we cannot charge admission for these performances and thus we have no box-office income. Even if a token admission is charged, the income will be negligible. We have not raised our full budget and most of the money we have raised must go for production costs.

We would still very much like to audition you, but I feel that you should know the situation as it is.

Subsistence pay would be enough to cover room, board and some spending money. It may even be necessary for you to find some part-time work in New Orleans. When on tour, the theater will take care of all expenses.

We hope to raise additional money during the latter part of the summer and throughout the year. Prospects are hopeful and when money becomes available we shall increase our salaries until they reach the Equity scale ($72.50 per week).

If you feel that you would still like to work with us in creating the Free Southern Theater, please let me know at your earliest convenience so that I might set up an appointment for an interview and audition.

Richard Schechner,
Producing Director

RS JO'N *Murray Levy was the first to join us, as actor and bookkeeper. As a veteran of ten years in the New York theater, both on and off Broadway, his political judgment brought him to disgust with the "New York experience" and led him, through Joy Manhoff, to the FST. . . .*

For almost three years Murray was, as nearly as I can understand, a Jewish Black Nationalist. He has recently returned to a posture more nearly resembling a more comfortable Marxism. But he is first of all an actor.

September 1964

Dear Joy,

Well I've been here for about ten days now and there are so many impressions, so much to be encouraged by and really not so much in the way of discouragement. But as we are all so eager to get going full steam ahead, the discouragements seem to get magnified.

Right off the bat let me say that I love New Orleans and that between Richard, Gilbert and me, the theater will get started. Today we opened our account in New Orleans with $3,500.00 and will be able to keep better books. I've been through the books from Tougaloo and all the money spent to date is accountable and none was spent for fripperies. I have everything itemized and any further expenses have to go through me. I was a bit miffed at FST's paying for Peter's flight to N.Y.—never again.

We were all disappointed about Abigail [Rosen, an actress who was expected to join the company but never did]. I hope that Jim Cromwell [a director recruit from N.Y.] gets here before Monday.

We are now concentrating on finding a home—a theater. It is more difficult than one might think, what with our being integrated and all. But there are some excellent local people now on our side who want to work with the theater. We charm most of the people (liberals) we meet and every sign points to big community interest.

I am rooming with John in a $40.00 a month flat which is really big enough for Cromwell too, so I hope he likes the idea.

Monday can't come soon enough. I have outlined a tentative tour which will take us not only through Mississippi, but to Memphis and Birmingham. This way we will play 4 Southern states and will truly be a Southern Theater, not just a Mississippi theater. The route I outlined cuts down any backtracking and any wasted mileage. With modification, I think it will work. The bombings in McComb yesterday fill me with rage and I wish we were ready to play now. McComb I think will be our first stop. The plays excite me a great deal. Especially *Godot.* The Moseses are great—we seem to be on the same radar beam—ditto with Richard. That is really more than I expected to find here.

It is very hot in New Orleans and the sun is merciless.

Living here is like living in a Utrillo painting and I'm sure you would love it. Erika Munk is very generous with her home and lets us use everything she owns.

As soon as I can I shall send you an up-to-date news release which, if you can, please try to get into the newspapers, not only in N.Y., but all over the country. We should be able to blanket the country with news of our activity. We shall see.

We had a mild demonstration when Goldwater spoke here—in the North it wouldn't even be considered a demonstration, but here they threatened and spat at us—nobody hurt. Did you ever see 35,000 shit heads sing "Dixie"—it's quite a sight.

Anyway, I hope you are well—and that your trip to L.A. was nice and that you think of us a lot. Wish you were nearby so I could visit or call.

Best to Bill—if you see Diana Sands give her my love—

Love to you,
Murray

GM *The FST was now composed of five members: John and myself, Richard Schechner, Denise Nicholas, and Murray Levy. Penny Hartzell, who had heard of FST in St. Louis, was on her way to join us, contacting various freedom projects en route to set up advance performance dates. Peter de Rome and Stanley Taylor, technical recruits from Mississippi and Manhattan, were also en route, along with Grace Brooks, a speech and drama teacher from Charleston, South Carolina. We were still completely integrated, from the company to the local board of directors to (in New Orleans) our audiences. Severn Darden, a Second City actor, came down with his wife Ann, and with James Cromwell comprised the "visiting director" staff. (Severn's father had been a city official in New Orleans, and he handled that ticklish situation by becoming "Carter Whitney" during his stay with us. Carter Whitney became the standard FST joke.)*

Through all our discussions—we had company meetings almost daily in those days—ran a fear of becoming "institutionalized," of succumbing to the establishment's structures in order to be funded by it, of becoming "bringers of culture to the masses." In trying to do its own thing, the FST was beginning to be caught in a trick bag.

RS *We planned three productions for our second tour:* Purlie Victorious, Waiting for Godot, *and Severn's improvisational show* The South Shall Rise Again. *But we hadn't yet found a permanent home. We were obliged to rehearse at first in our own apartments; then later the pastors of two black churches offered us their halls for rehearsal.*

The details of our "theater" had to be taken care of as with any theater: Where could we get a car for the tour, by what date could we have our plays ready and where would we take them, should we or should we not play New York in a series of fund-raising benefits the New York people were pressuring us to give, where were our salaries going to come from, how could we "organize" more efficiently?

September 22, 1964

Dear Gil,

I may reach you in New Orleans before this does, but in any case all this information will get recorded.

Enclosed is a list of all the projects that I contacted, both those that received a performance of *In White America* and those that did not. The list includes the people we should keep in contact with (never using COFO in the address) and the addresses. There is a definite interest among these projects (numbering 23), and they can find some type of building for us to perform in. They of course all want to know as soon as we can tell them the date or dates that we will be there.

Holly Springs said that *after the middle of November would be best because cotton picking season would be over,* but that this is not imperative. Also added that the area is a large one and they could use two performances.

I also talked to Bill Hutchinson. He seemed to think that the beginning of December until the 19th (any time in there) would be better for the Theater Festival at Tougaloo; I think he's planning one of Tougaloo's play productions for the November date that you gave me. He naturally wants to know what you have planned for the Festival and what you expect him to do.

You also asked what the Movement has planned. I haven't talked to Jessie Morris yet; I will. It seems that November will be involved with campaigning though it occurs to me that the election will be November 3. Voter registration and community centers are continuing and the school children usually go there after school. None of the places expressed November and December as inconvenient months to come, although they all said that advanced notices would be appreciated in order to give them a chance for publicity.

That's the report from this end.

See you soon!
Penny

MINUTES
Free Southern Theater Company Meeting
October 5, 1964

Attended by: Gil Moses, John O'Neal, Murray Levy, James Cromwell, Peter de Rome, Grace Brooks, Penelope Hartzell [secretary].

Company meetings will be held every Saturday at 1:00 P.M. We shall meet outside Richard Schechner's office at Tulane University.

Gil Moses explained the organization of the corporation and the function of the Sponsors and Board of Directors. The Board of Directors, as in any corporation, gives the necessary air of respectability to the organization. Gil raised the question whether or not Richard had gotten letters off to James Forman and Fannie Lou Hamer asking them to become members of the Board of Directors.

Elizabeth Sutherland, of the *Nation,* has written asking FST to write and/or act in a history of SNCC for the SNCC anniversary celebration in NYC this February 1. We decided it was impossible for any of us to write such a play or to rehearse for one written by anyone else. Penny will write Elizabeth and tell her what we are doing, ask her how much time in the program we would have, suggest that we do a part or all of *Purlie,* and ask her what the plans involve and what we could do other than a SNCC history.

John O'Neal stated that it was not fitting or appropriate for FST to play outside (of the South). Were we to mishandle our responsibility to our Mississippi audience we would lose our distinctive quality and our fund-raising potential as the group we are. If FST goes to NYC untested and without having found our material and our identity we would subject ourselves to a critical evaluation which is not right. NYC would miss the point of FST, witnessing it separated from its audience.

Murray Levy added that it is tempting and romantic to go to NYC, and that he agreed with John.

Gil Moses pointed out that the point of going to NYC is to raise money by doing benefits and that he too is waiting for FST to develop its own style and material, but the first is a practical consideration; the second, a philosophical one.

Murray added that going to NYC might also attract Negro actors and actresses whom we need badly.

John said that we should get them to come to us rather than us to them.

Murray and James stated that we do not have the name to draw them here.

John said he was willing to accept the possibility of going to NYC to raise money.

The length of the tour was decided to go to January 30 if it is needed and to break for at least 10 days for Christmas vacation. It was requested that we break and reassemble in a fairly large city which has easy transportation connections. James said that it was not necessary to plan for too many days off during the tour and we agreed that one day a week is enough.

Route 3, Box 83
Carthage, Mississippi
Octomber 2, 1964

Dear John and Penny,

We would like for you to bring your play to Carthage at the set date January 17 . . . the community center will be open for your show, and accomodations will be arranged for the characters.

Sincerely yours,
Annie and Theodis
COFO

October 9, 1964

Sandy Leigh
507 Mobile Street
Hattiesburg, Mississippi

Dear Sandy,

The Free Southern Theater will tour Mississippi, Memphis, Atlanta, and Birmingham with *Purlie Victorious* and *Waiting for Godot* during November, December, and January. We would like to play in HATTIESBURG on SATURDAY AND SUNDAY, JANUARY 23 and 24.

Please reply immediately as to the convenience of these dates, the place you have in mind for us to perform in, its size, and the accommodations you can arrange for our thirteen players (eight men and five women). It is important that we hear from you right away so we can make adjustments if necessary.

We will inform you of further developments, publicity, etc. directly we hear from all projects. A reply card is enclosed for your convenience.

Sincerely,
John O'Neal and Penny Hartzell

Hattiesburg, Mississippi
12 Oct 64

Dear John, Penny, *et al:*

Y'all come anytime you want. Give us about a month for publicity. Accomodations always available. Couldn't think about an engagement around the holiday season, could you? Come to think of it, WHY ARE WE ON THE BOTTOM OF THE LIST??? (Just joking. I know about the schedules and all.)

Anticipating, and so on . . .
Sandy Leigh and the H'burgers

MINUTES
Third Free Southern Theater Company Meeting
October 17, 1964

Attended by: Gilbert Moses, Richard Schechner, John O'Neal, James Cromwell, Murray Levy, Grace Brooks, Severn Darden alias Carter Whitney alias Henry Brown, Penny Hartzell [secretary], and Joe Hanlan.

Monday night, October 19, the first board meeting will be held at Richard Schechner's apartment. Denise Moses will be secretary. The by-laws will be decided so that tax exemption can be applied for.

Richard sent a progress report of FST to the Rockefeller Foundation. A carbon will be kept on file and Richard will sharpen and shorten it to be duplicated and we will send it out to important money people as a newsletter. Joy Manhoff will talk to the Ford Foundation people personally.

We received a letter from Langston Hughes.

Joy sent a letter requesting that some of the company go to NYC over Christmas to talk to money people; she also said that *Life* wants to do a feature on FST and that we should not get a professional fund raiser; that they are doing as good as one could.

Severn Darden said that the week the *Life* article [a theater review of FST] comes out is the best time for fund raising and if we request it *Life* will tell us previously the week it will be published so we can get ready.

The plans for building the screens are ready. If we can get the money for the screens from the Board we will build them, if not we will do without. Same goes for the ground cloth. Denise will mobilize a crew and find a place to build them on Saturday, October 23.

Peter de Rome is leaving the company due to unexpected circumstances. Stanley Taylor will be stage manager for *Purlie,* Grace will be stage manager for *Godot,* Denise will head up publicity with Stanley as her assistant, and Penny will take care of other letter writing.

The idea of doing a benefit at the Royal Art movie house will be brought up at the Board meeting.

The Tulane Wesley Foundation asked us to play at the Louisiana Methodist Student Movement Conference to be held February 19–21. We decided to do it for room, board, travel and $100. If they don't give us travel then $150.

The Brandeis Women will give us a benefit when we perform for them at the end of February, Richard announced. This will be excellent for some money.

John asked about playing Louisiana for CORE there. It was decided to make excursions out after we return from the tour and while we are rehearsing the new play.

It was decided to pass the hat at Atlanta when we play there on tour.

Dear Gang,

The dates you mention for being in Greenville and surrounding area are fine with us. People here are still talking about your last play, so I think they will be delighted to hear that you are returning. Will let you know as soon as we have a definite place for you to perform (we have something up our sleeve which will be confirmed early this week). One question: (will both plays be given on the same night or one on each night?)

Pat Vail
Greenville Project

Dear John,

Sorry to be a bit late answering your letter. We will have a place for you on January 18th and 19th and will do some posters to assure you an audience. The place we have in mind will hold about 300 people. We will make arrangements for places for the cast to sleep. Men may have to sleep on the floor at the Freedom House but we'll try to do better than that.

Regards to the Mosii.

Eric Weinberger

Dear Penny,

We received your letter and will be expecting you on the 28 and 29 of November.

Unfortunately our Freedom School was damaged by a fire and you will not be able to use it for your presentation. Instead you will have to use St. Benedict the Moor Recreation Center which has a stage of about 40′ × 20′. You will be able to use this place on the twenty-ninth. On the twenty-eighth you will be able to perform in Williams Chapel in Ruleville, Miss. The stage there is about 30′ × 10′.

When you get into Sunflower County please come to Indianola first as your housing for the two days will be there.

Please send details about the two plays immediately to me so I can start publicizing the two plays.

Yours in Freedom,
Fred B. Winn

MINUTES
Fourth Free Southern Theater Company Meeting
October 24, 1964

Attended by: Gilbert Moses, John O'Neal, Richard Schechner, James Cromwell, Murray Levy, Stanley Taylor, Severn Darden, Grace Brooks, Denise Moses, and Penny Hartzell [secretary].

The new New Orleans opening dates are as follows:

November	11	*Purlie*	St. John's
	12	*Godot*	St. John's
	13	*Godot*	Dillard
	14	*Godot*	matinee benefit place unknown
	14	*Purlie*	New Zion
	16	*Improvisations*	Central Congregational
	17	*Improvisations*	place unknown

Richard said that some research should be done into the costs, insurance, etc. of purchasing a truck. John added that we also need a new license for the Plymouth because the Mississippi one will expire soon. It was agreed that we should get a Louisiana license plate for the Plymouth and that as many people as possible should get La. drivers' licenses. John agreed to handle the research and the getting of La. plates for the Plymouth.

The rights for *Purlie* will be $10 a performance. A second letter has been sent to Grove Press about *Godot* for we have heard nothing.

Tools: Richard read the list of tools needed for building the screens and recommended we buy staple gun, folding rule, tape rule, pliers, and a large screw driver. Stanley will see if the carpenter has the other needed tools, and Richard will take whatever else we need from the Tulane theater shop. The screens will be built at St. John's in the evenings beginning Thursday. Richard will learn on Monday whether or not Mr. Mervis (of the Board) can get the building materials except for burlap free. If he cannot, we will not build the screens. Gil will draw up plans for building a collapsible coffin to be used in *Purlie* and he will pass it on to Richard for Brooks MacNamera to look at. Stanley is in charge of getting the screens built.

We are in dire need of a secretarial assistant! Richard will put an article in the Tulane paper.

Publicity: Mike Sayer will do flyers for free, but it is so close to opening and the dates keep shifting that it will be necessary to get them printed in New Orleans. Denise will go to the Times-P. about getting a running article in that paper about FST and the plays. Mel Leavitt should be contacted about filming stuff for TV. Matt Herron is coming to rehearsals to take rehearsal shots. It was suggested by Rev. Hausey at St. John's that we call the Urban League to obtain a list of the Negro churches to send flyers to. Denise has written a blurb to give the college papers and Rev. Hausey's newsletter. John said that Oretha knows of some funeral homes, etc. that have offset presses who are willing to let them be used for free.

Severn said that Paul Sills is willing to come down for 10 days to help him get the improvisation show off its feet. He will pay his transportation if FST will pay the $30 train fare back to Chicago.

Denise was supposed to speak at the Liberals Club Monday night about FST, but she has rehearsal. Gil, James, and Murray will go instead since they are not needed for the first hour. Richard will pick up the rest of the cast for rehearsal.

John suggested that we need an up-to-date brochure, a sort of continuation of the *TDR* ad, with info about the company. Gil said that it is not essential now and besides we don't have the time or money to get one printed.

Murray said that the benefit cannot be held in NYC on Nov. 22 because it is the anniversary of Kennedy's murder; therefore, it has been temporarily held up until another date opens up.

Richard asked if he can explore the possibility of getting the theater from Kazan and Whitehead for February. He was given the go ahead for dates between Feb. 1 and 14. Murray said that Arthur Kinoy, a civil rights lawyer friend from NYC, said we would be able to raise a bundle of money in NYC.

Denise said that anyone who wants can write an article for *Players Magazine;* they want one. Richard is planning an interview article for *TDR* for the June issue. Gil said that *Harpers* has asked him to write an article for a spring issue on the South.

November 4, 1964

Dear Free Southern Theater,

We have procured the Friendship Baptist Church for your thespial endeavor on the dates which you specified (we tried to get one of the high schools, but the superintendent preferred that we leave town). This is the same church which you used this past summer.

The housing is taken care of—tent city.

STRUGGLING,
Pat Vail
Greenville Project

Fall 1964

Dear Joy,

Since writing last Hilda has been here for a brief appearance, left a few buildings torn down and travelled along. It was, for many of us, our first hurricane.

Cromwell is an extraordinary director. His attack on *Godot* is so very actable and Gilbert (DiDi) and I (GoGo) are doing some of the best work I have ever seen at any rehearsal. For a while we experimented with different people trying all the parts and now the casting is set.

Penny and Grace have done a great job getting the files in order. It's all so fucking organized that I may throw up. You know dear heart that I function best in the midst of chaos.

Anyway, with both plays going full steam ahead, the files and money matters all squared away (unlike the big time, we discourage the passing around of ice), the tour itself almost plotted, promises of help with publicity from Tulane students and CORE people, two great rehearsal places to work in, it really feels like we are a theater company. This is how we do it:

9:00 A.M.	everybody up
10:00 A.M.	Company meeting
11:00 A.M.	*Godot* rehearsal
4:00	Break for dinner
7:00	*Purlie* rehearsal
10:00	Quittin' time

We follow this schedule Monday through Friday, and on weekends we let it happen as it will. That is, we do the scenes that need the work on the weekends.

John just had a wisdom tooth removed and is just getting over it today. That's all for this minute.

Murray

MINUTES
Fifth Free Southern Theater Company Meeting
November 7, 1964

Attended by: Gilbert Moses, John O'Neal, Richard Schechner, James Cromwell, Murray Levy, Stanley Taylor, Grace Brooks,

Denise Moses, Cynthia Small [newly recruited as office manager and actress], Ann Darden, and Penny Hartzell.

Truck Report: John said that we can get a car at greatly reduced rate at Bill Spiro's in Memphis. He sells his cars to SNCC and we would purchase through SNCC. We can get a station wagon just like the one we have now; someone would have to go pick it up. James said that he doesn't think we should get a 6-cylinder car and that buses don't hold the road. He recommended a 9-passenger station wagon plus a U-Haul. The rent on a U-Haul, however, does not make it worthwhile, said Ann Darden. John thought one more 6-passenger wagon would be enough, but after discussion of how much we have to carry with us: flats, tree, mound, lights, light stands, etc., it was agreed that a bus would be the best thing. Ann Darden will take care of getting the Plymouth fixed, purchasing a bus from Spiro through SNCC, getting the Louisiana license plate. It was stressed that everyone should get Louisiana driver's licenses.

Murray asked how people wanted to get paid on tour: the full $35 each week or subsistence with the balance right before vacation. The count was so split that Murray said he will give everyone full salary to make his work easier. When Richard arrived after class he suggested that we get paid during Christmas vacation for we aren't getting that much money anyway and there may be things we want to do. At one point it was suggested that each of us take a cut in salary when we go on tour because we don't need as much money in Mississippi while touring. But Gilbert said that the socialistic system of getting what one needs when one needs it doesn't work. Thus each will get a regular salary from which he must take care of *all* his needs. Some were reluctant about getting paid over Christmas vacation because we don't have that much funds, so it was decided at Richard's suggestion that those who don't want their pay can give it back to FST when Murray gives out the salary.

Stanley asked about bond if we're thrown in jail. Richard said FST has telephone numbers of lawyers in New Orleans who

RICHARD PIPES

Robert Costley (left) and Gary Bolling at Texas Southern University, July, 1967

TOM WAKAYAMA

Grace Brooks and John O'Neal in PURLIE VICTORIOUS, Winter, 1964–65

RICHARD PIPES

Cynthia McPherson and Gary Bolling in *An Evening of Afro-American Poetry* at Texas Southern University, July, 1967

MATT HERRON

Lester Gault, Holmes County, Miss., Summer, 1964

Murray Levy and Jaci Earley in THE LESSON at Tuskeegee Institute, July, 1967

(left to right) Murray Levy, Emalyn Hawkins, Roscoe Orman and Gilbert Moses in THE RIFLES OF SENORA CARRAR, New Orleans, Summer, 1965

RICHARD PIPES

Roscoe Orman, Robert Costley (partly obscured) and Denise Nicholas in rehearsal of IN WHITE AMERICA, New Orleans, Summer, 1965

BOB FLETCHER

Murray Levy in IN WHITE AMERICA, Summer, 1965

John Cannon and Roscoe O[illegible]
man in IN WHITE AMERI[illegible]
Summer, 1964

BOB FLETC[illegible]

MATT HERRON

James Cromwell, Murray Levy and Gilbert Moses in WAITING FOR GODOT, Ruleville, Miss., Fall, 1964

(left to right) Jaci Earley, Gary Bolling and Cynthia McPherson in HAPPY ENDING, LeMoyne College, Memphis, Tenn., June, 1967

BOB FLETCHER

DENNIS J. CIPNIC

Tom Dent leading discussion at Free Southern Theater building, GHETTO OF DESIRE TV show, June, 1966

ROBERT ANALAUAGE

Denise Nicholas and Joseph Perry in DOES MAN HELP MAN, Bethel Lutheran Church, New Orleans, August, 1966

Murray Levy during rehearsal at New Orleans, Summer, 1965

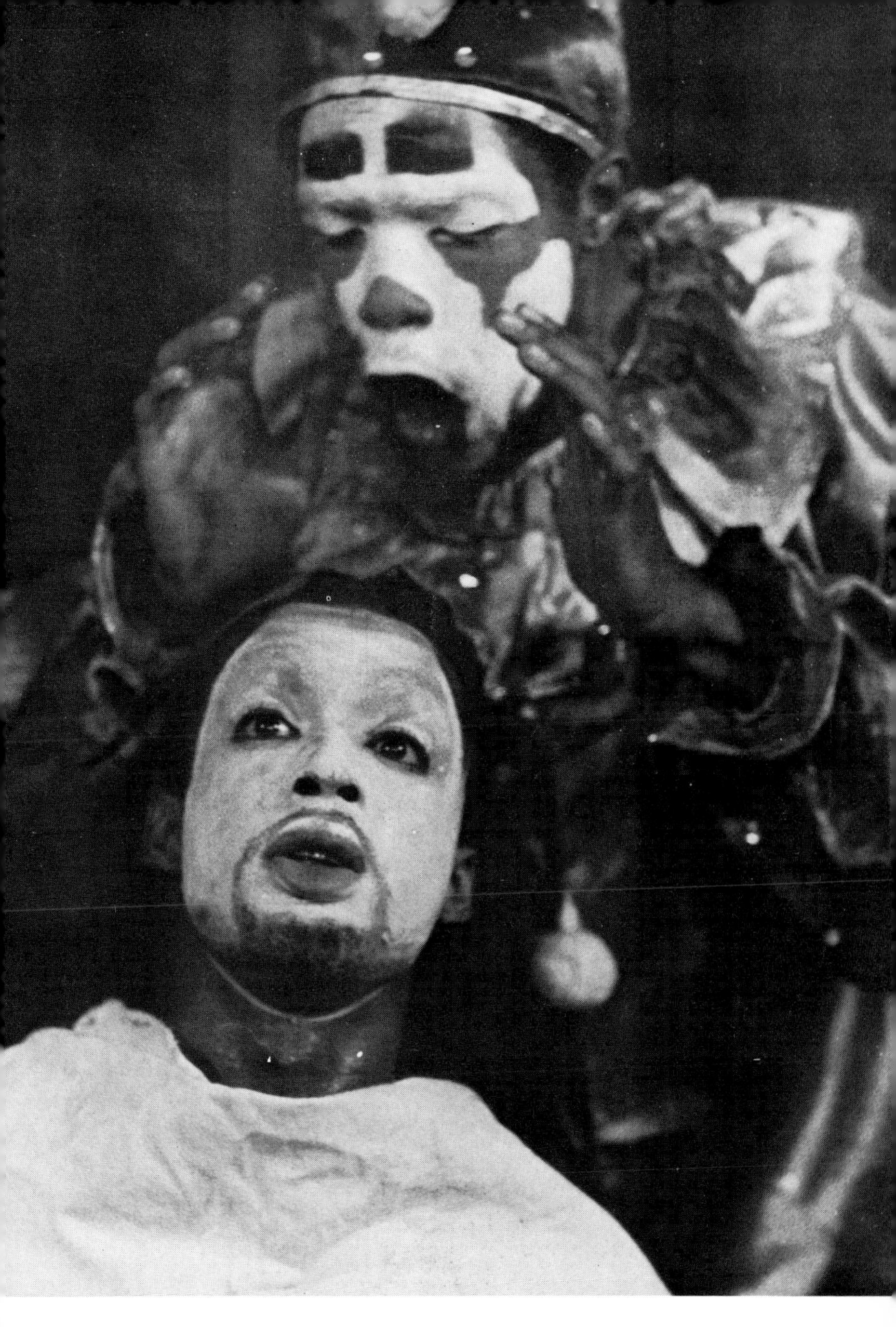

oscoe Orman (top) and Joseph Perry in DOES MAN HELP MAN, Bethel
utheran Church, New Orleans, August, 1966

DENNIS J. CIPN

Denise Nicholas at GHETTO OF DESIRE TV poetry show, New Orleans, June, 1966

(left to right) Gilbert Moses, Roger Johnson, John O'Neal, Holmes County, Miss., Summer, 1964

MATT HERR

will help us. Gilbert added that FST will take care of everybody and Denise added that we will all have a tour-orientation session to go through before we leave.

John said that Peter Garrison, treasurer for the Board of Directors, looked at our books. They are a good informal record, but he will set up more formal books which the part-time secretary can take care of. He suggested that since we are not stable financially, we maintain a frequent audit. In addition statements must be submitted to internal revenue on a monthly basis. We are already two months behind on that and we can be arrested for tax evasion.

MINUTES
Orientation for Mississippi Company Meeting
November 19, 1964, New Orleans

DISCIPLINE: James said that violence and being late should be fined. He's suggesting warning and then fine. Warned if you're late for half-hour, fined $2.50 if late for places. John doesn't think fines will help. Denise said that we have to commit ourselves to the theater on tour, thus we will have NO excuse for being late and the fines will work. Gil agreed. As a producing director the commitment is to the show. Richard opposed to fines; it has potential of tearing the group apart. Rehearsal lateness: $2.50, performance, $5.00; crew call and violence, $5.00.

JOB ALLOTMENTS: *Purlie* lights, Stanley; set including furniture, Gil and James; props, Grace; costumes, dressing room, and make-up, Penny; house, programs, questionnaires, community relations, housing, Denise. John will be at Denise's disposal for community relations.

DRIVERS: Gil, Penny, John, James, Grace. John will be in charge of the fleet.

PROCEDURE: Set up first, eating secondary. Everyone must check with stage manager before leaving finished job. (1) unload, (2) set up house, (3) set up stage. Gil is in charge of reblocking *Purlie* while on tour. Stanley take care of exit and entrance rehearsal. *Godot* Stanley and John will redo set at direction of James. Stanley and James and John on lights for this. Strike and pack after *Godot* so ready to leave in morning.

MISSISSIPPI ORIENTATION: Local people you must look out for; cops have not been responsible for harassment. Don't feel bad about being scared, but don't let it show. Radio procedure will be learned at McComb. The call number is KUY 1104. Everyone will have Richard's, Cynthia's and Lolis Elie's numbers. Always call the COFO office of the town you are in if arrested and tell them to start the machinery rolling. Don't go anywhere alone; tell the stage manager where you are going; play it by ear; don't antagonize.

Mississippi is a dry state; never have alcohol on your person.

Some places have curfews; this must be followed closely. Don't be deceived by the attitude of the COFO people. Travelling in integrated groups is OK. Miss. has become inured and one purpose is to show people integration. Politeness is important. All the time two travel together. 6:00 call for costume and make-up.

Penny: There is no clearly understood goal of FST; when we get to New York, I am sure we each will tell people different things because we don't know and we have our own ideas.

James: We need a definition of a free theater, Southern theater, and free Southern theater in Mississippi. I feel Miss. is involved in a revolution and revolution is no time for theater. It must be a new thing completely different that develops out of revolution. Theater, established, comes after the revolution. This new thing must come from the revolution. FST is not free—it is begging with its green bowl in the back of every place we play in. Free theater becomes charity and people have too much pride to accept charity. I think they need *In White America* which gives them faith to go through what they're doing. FST isn't Southern because it isn't supported by the South.

John: We need to consider the program that is needed in the community and to become a professional touring company.

James: In all the criticisms and problems we have the revolution and we have the theater and they keep bumping into each other in FST.

John: Can we define these two things?

1964–1965

Purlie Victorious
by Ossie Davis

Waiting for Godot
by Samuel Becket

Company

Gilbert Moses—producer, actor
John O'Neal—producer, actor
Richard Schechner—producer, director (*Purlie*)
James Cromwell—director (*Godot*), actor
Grace Brooks—actress
Penny Hartzell—actress
Stanley Taylor—stage manager, actor
Denise Nicholas—actress, office staff
Murray Levy—actor, business manager
Severn Darden—improvisation and acting coach
Paul Sills—improvisation coach
Peter de Rome—actor, publicity
Cynthia Small—office staff

Tour Schedule

November 11–17—New Orleans, La.
November 20–21—McComb, Miss.

November 23–24—Vicksburg, Miss.
November 25–26—Greenville, Miss.
November 27–28—Ruleville, Miss.
November 29–30—Indianola, Miss.
December 2–3 —Canton, Miss.
December 4–5 —Tougaloo College, Miss.
December 6–7 —Mileston, Miss. (Tchula)
December 8–9 —Greenwood, Miss.
December 10–11—Mound Bayou, Miss.
December 12–13—Clarksdale, Miss.
December 15–16—Batesville, Miss.
December 17–18—Holly Springs, Miss.
December 19–20—Memphis, Tenn.
January 3–7 —Atlanta, Georgia
January 8 —Aberdeen, Miss.
January 9 —West Point, Miss.
January 10 —Columbus, Miss.
January 11–12 —Meridian, Miss.
January 13–14 —Carthage, Miss.
January 15–19 —Jackson, Miss.
January 21–22 —Laurel, Miss.
January 23–24 —Hattiesburg, Miss.
January 25–26 —Moss Point, Miss.
January 27–28 —Gulfpoint, Miss.
February 5 —New York City, New School for Social Research
February 12 —New York City, American Place Theater

GM *Opened our two plays (the improvisational show had been canceled) to full houses at St. John's Institutional Baptist Church.* Purlie *laid the audience in the aisles with laughter.* Godot *mystified, amused, bored, shocked them.*

In Clarksdale, Miss., James Cromwell played Pozzo in blackface, provoking concentrated audience attention. In Greenville,

Miss., kids threw spitballs during the second act of Godot, *and in Indianola, Miss., Gitlow, in* Purlie, *entered on stage from the cotton field, with cotton bolls dropping from his overalls.*

In Mileston, Miss., during the discussion after the presentation of Godot, *one man asked, "When Pozzo puts the cap on Lucky's head to make him think, does that mean that the FST wants to put the thinking cap on us?"*

Waiting for Godot
Williams Chapel
Ruleville, Mississippi
November 28, 1964

Program Notes:

House about 45.

Babies in audience.

Chuckles right away at Murray trying to take off his boot; "Now you got it," a man in the audience said at one point.

Chuckles at Murray replying to Didi that he slept "in a ditch."

A few laughs at Didi telling Gogo "You wouldn't go far" when Gogo says he would like it better alone.

Quite a big laugh when Gogo asks Pozzo for his bones.

A lady in the audience said, "He wants another bone," when Gogo tells Pozzo he's in no hurry to leave.

Laughter at Stanley every time he backs away from Didi in fear.

Mrs. Fannie Lou Hamer spoke during intermission (without our requesting it) and told the audience that turkeys and other food would be sent down from Chicago to Mississippi. Then she said that she had come back from Chicago in order to see Gil Moses and the Free Southern Theater and that everyone should pay strict attention to the play because it's due to waiting that the Negro is as far behind as he is.

Great laugh on "You piss better when I'm not with you."

Discussion Notes:

Fannie Lou Hamer: It's somewhat similar to any person in a suffering condition who just keeps on waiting and nothing happens.

Pozzo & Lucky: It looks like Pozzo took advantage of Lucky.

A Negro woman: He was the master and Lucky was the slave.

FLH: No matter how tired he was he had to do it right off the bat, but he (Lucky) didn't like it. He (Lucky) was afraid to take the rope off.

Negro woman: Why didn't he take it off when he had a chance?

Young Negro girl: Lucky feels pity for him because he (Pozzo) was blind.

FLH: Sometimes regardless how hard it be you have pity for someone.

Negro woman: Maybe in this race relation business we should take the rope off our necks after the master goes blind. Who is Godot? Where does he fit in? Was the boy Stanley playing different? Was he the same?

FLH: I figured you were the second brother. You was certainly looking the same way. I feel it's important for us to point out for ourselves about ropes and things. You can do this play for the next fifty years and there'll be people waiting. I've seen old men; I've seen people like you and they weren't acting; sometimes a whole bench of people on the street and one pats another on the back and asks what you're doing and he says nothin'. Not actin', just this natural, with clothes like these clothes. There ain't too many people in Mississippi who can see it like us. . . . Just like John O'Neal said (in *Purlie* third act) he was murdering him (Ol' Cap'n) in his heart.

When we asked for a place for the Moseses to stay that night FLH replied, "My house is a sad case but you're welcome to stay. It's one of those three room huts that looks like I'm waiting."

(Letter to the New York Fund-Raising Committee
December 11, 1964)

Our plays have been presented under all imaginable conditions.

Last month in Indianola we gave an outside afternoon performance of PURLIE VICTORIOUS. We set up our playing area on a field next to the Indianola Freedom School which had recently been condemned by city officials due to a fire which had "mysteriously" broken out in the building. COFO workers say that firemen watched the building burn, and that after finally deciding to put the fire out, they destroyed a lot of equipment in the building with water hoses and axes.

During the two hours it took us to set up we attracted a crowd of over 200 people. We invited children to help us lash our flats. The atmosphere was of a circus where actors and their make-up were the attractions. The outdoor setting was especially appropriate for the character Gitlow who, for the first time, literally ran on stage from the cotton field spewing cotton from his pockets. That afternoon performance was one of the most exhilarating thus far.

Questions from the people after the performance rejuvenate us. Of course, there are some who listen to the discussion much in the same manner that they have watched the play; there are some who wait on others to formulate their thought. But there are those who ask a lot of questions, who have a great deal to say . . .

The Free Southern Theater exists for all the people here, and in particular for those people who are just beginning to express themselves.

We arrived in Mound Bayou yesterday morning, the only all-Negro community in Mississippi. It was raining. The rain had washed the dirt roads clean to the gravel underneath, filling the deep draining ditches on both sides, churning the dirt roads into mud moats.

Entering the COFO office here, we saw some local people filling out forms to receive old clothes. They said, "We're coming to the performance tonight." In the rain, driving in their trucks for miles to come to our church/theater, over muddy roads, they come.

For these people, and for us, we extend our thanks.

Respectfully,
The Free Southern Theater Company

From Penny Hartzell's Journal

December 16–22, 1964

We must seriously consider staying five days in each town on the next tour. In two days we can get slightly acquainted with the people with whom we stay, but not with the community. This not only prevents us from knowing what they think about the plays, but from having any diversions. We spend so much time together it is no wonder we often get on each other's nerves. At the same time the group becomes a refuge for me from going out and meeting people on my own. I never knew I could be so reluctant to meet people who are not from a culture that I know. What do I talk about with a farmer's wife who has lived around Mileston, Mississippi, all her 45 years, who replies, when I say I went to school in Indiana, "Chicago, Indiana?" What to say does not go through my mind while I sit at the kitchen table with her. All I have is a distinct feeling of curiosity mixed with hesitation and an empty mind. Grace seems to find it simpler; she can talk to these people about nothing for a long time—chitchat, small talk. Still, the theater must come from these people; they are the ones who come to see the plays. I know everyone can't be wildly enthusiastic like Jerry in Ruleville who sneaked up on stage with a buddy after the play and got on Pozzo's costume and put the rope around his friend's neck and shouted "On" and went through many of the lines from memory after seeing a rehearsal and one performance.

And can we really expect more than a blasé acceptance of the plays such as we received in Greenville? I assume they'll all come running, thrilled to death at the opportunity to see some live theater performed especially for them. Although that is the case in quite a few towns, should it be for all of them? As we have observed, the audiences are more excited about us in the rural towns of under 10,000 people than in the larger ones of 20,000.

Can we ever realize with what eyes and thoughts these people approach *Purlie Victorious* and *Waiting for Godot*? After the play is over we seldom hear the words "drama" and "theater." Some refer to it as "the meeting," others say they thought it was going to be a movie and were surprised to see live people up there. Some are captivated by the reality of the thing. (Eating real sweet potato pie, smoking, and eating chicken.) All of this before their eyes excites them very much. The difference between their make-believe (TV and the movies) and real life becomes blurred during the plays. That's why, possibly, they usually don't bother to listen to Pozzo. He is the white master and one need go no further than that; what could he possibly say to interest them? But when James put on the blackface in Clarksdale the audience paid him some attention for he was an unusual, strange character they couldn't figure out. It seems that the first physical appearance and words of a character are most important, and determine the amount of attention the audience will pay him after that.

We have taken on an enormous task. We need people who are committed for at least a year or two to making this thing work. The experience we eight are gaining on this tour will be put into use on the next tour, which hopefully will be better and will make more progress. But if most of us leave after the year is out that means training new people. . . .

January 2, 1965, Atlanta

Tonight James asked me if I thought we should go to NYC. I told him I didn't think we were good enough. He agreed. We talked a long while about FST morale, discipline, talent, and art. . . .

I don't know what can be done about going to NYC. I am afraid that going to NYC and giving a bad showing will only discourage those who might continue to support us. We need that support and we'd all be better off if the FST went when it was ready, when we could face the New York audience, the people whose judgment and art we respect. One reason we lag may be the dissipation of energy due to the jobs we have in addition to acting and the theater work. If we get a front man to take the publicity, tour, and housing arrangements and if we could have a technician or two it would make life simpler in one respect, but the additional people would be impossible to handle at this point.

Company meeting, January 3, 1965
Atlanta, Georgia

Fines will come out of the salary rather than from Murray following people around to collect. Gil, Denise, Murray, John, and Stanley were late arriving; John was late for rehearsal.

John would like to hold a hearing on his last fine. He ran into bad weather. He left Chicago at 4 P.M. anticipating an 18-hour drive; it took him 24 hours. He had allowed three extra hours. He did not call in to say that he was going to be late. Vote: James no, Grace says either all will be fined or none, Denise agrees. Stanley says he detests lateness and he votes to fine everyone including himself; he doesn't want to know all the personal reasons. Murray no, Denise yes, Penny yes, Stanley no, Gil no. No fine for John.

John was late this afternoon because he thought we were

coming to Frank Smith's [a SNCC worker] wedding and he had to get a ride when he could. All except Stanley voted fine on this.

Gil and Denise for missing airplane; all vote fine except Murray who abstained.

Murray for missing airplane; he was depending upon Gil and Denise to get him up. John no, James yes, Grace yes, Penny yes, Denise yes, Stanley yes, Gil abstained.

Stanley for staying because his mother was sick and thus not arriving on time. John no, James no, Grace no, Murray no, Denise no, Penny abstained, Gil yes.

John suggested having rewards for meritorious service; e.g. for Murray running around NYC getting makeup and costumes during Christmas. This idea rejected.

James is against going to NYC and especially against playing in Harlem. He, as a director, does not think *Waiting for Godot* is ready. And Harlem would not judge the theater objectively anyway.

Murray thinks if we don't play NYC for the reasons James says then we shouldn't play in Mississippi either. The only reason that he doesn't want to play NYC is because he doesn't have anything he wants to say to NYC.

Denise said Murray is assuming a lot about the company. We are a group of people who have come together to form a theater; we are in our fourth month; we are untrained for the most part.

Gil does not think we should go to NY. Recently he has felt we should not even finish this tour. The pilot tour did not teach him much; this one has taught more. We've learned what doesn't work; we know we need a front man; we need a new set and new direction for *Purlie;* we need another actor for Pozzo. "I think we should go back to New Orleans and like start anew and not even go on with the tour."

John said nobody has the right reason for not going to NYC, although he too thinks we should not go. He hopes no one is ever satisfied with his work. He reacts against the antiseptic purism that seems to be going on in everybody's minds. The reason for not going is that we would miss the commitment to theater we have in this place and that's why we shouldn't go to New York or anywhere else for that matter. We have to figure out what it means to have theater in this place. "I'm sure it means going out to the communities and establishing theaters; it means finishing the tour; it means dealing with our frustrations about the way FST is."

Gil said that we cannot decide not to play in NYC. We have to talk to Schechner and Carol Feinman. We can hold a forum at the New School for Social Research. Having photographs taken, talking to people. We're all going to NYC in any case, for various other reasons.

Murray doesn't want to have a forum at the New School—he would go to New York to play, because he's an actor, not a good chatter. He would rather go to New Orleans and work on the theater there.

Gil said that he is tired of making decisions and being a producer-director.

John said he told the people in Chicago that we're trying to do the impossible: to form a democratic theater.

James says that the democratic system doesn't work. . . .

Denise said, "I'm for good theater, and I don't think democratic theater works either."

Stanley said that he hopes the producing directors will consider getting a generator. Gil asked Denise to see about a generator.

John is going to be working on a community program in the spring.

Grace said one thing we need to do is either to go to Mississippi, even though the plays are bad, or to quit. We need someone looking at both sides to decide what to do. . . .

Discussion continued, nothing resolved.

RS *We ended the 1964 season by presenting* Godot *at the New School for Social Research, and* Purlie *at the American Place Theater, in New York. During our performance of* Godot *Murray, playing GoGo, spit at the audience as he delivered the line "What, in this muck heap?"*

Two FBI members allowed John O'Neal to finish the New School performance of Godot *before they arrested him as an "unproven" conscientious objector.*

From Penny Hartzell's Journal

February 1, 1965
New York City
7:30 A.M.
they sleep on

Depression and dejection: that poster printed by NAACP declares, "You can kill a man, but you can't kill an idea." James replied to it, "Bullshit." I, too, now say, "Bullshit." FST is a grand, good idea, but if the eight of us go, FST goes. The idea might survive us, but in the end what good is that? It has to be real and only men are real; ideas never are! There is a lot more to this idea-man business. The idea in the hands of competent people is one thing and the idea in the hands of nincompoops is another. Gil and John are the latter when it comes to theater. Who ever heard of two people beginning a theater and being part of the administration and the artistic staff when they didn't know anything about running a theater? . . . Under the best of conditions it takes time to form a repertory company that does fine work. How pretentious to come marching to New York City after being in existence for less than a year. But we are here and the article in the *New York Times* declares we are here (with a six-column article and pictures, too); and suddenly the farce of life hits with full force. What happened to art and the critical eye? Ah, but the performances haven't happened yet. Then perhaps justice will prevail.

Essentially I am torn. Should I chuck FST because I see its doom to failure just as I see the daylight outside? Or should I stick out another tour trying to make it work and learning more about the South, its people, and its problem, since I certainly won't learn more about theater? I know deep down the latter will prevail—I really haven't anything better to do and I hate quitting. But will this thing destroy me; that is the only thing I must be wary of. Being constantly "down" is not fun for me or for anyone else; it may not be worth it.

Then let us think of this: what if James who I think started a lot of the real discontent, or shall I say thinking, in FST, what if James were wrong? What if, through the confusion and frustration, a new theater, type of theater, were born? Is James' foisting off the standard ideas of how theater should be accomplished stultifying to people who don't know anything of these ideas and to some new "thing" which might grow from a naïve approach to theater? James is correct when he says that a professional touring company must do the theater that it knows and must stimulate the people (our audience) to create their own theater of needs and desires. That is the only theater James could be a part of; but John might be a part of the new "thing." Gil, I don't know—I guess all he really cares about is fame, else why would he be in New York? Does he honestly think the people of Mississippi and especially of Jackson, its capital, cannot afford to support a theater? Is that honestly why he is in New York trying to raise money? Or is he here because he can get his name in the paper and hobnob with the famous folk? It's a daring question to ask and a dangerous one to answer. I think I know how Gil feels; I was excited to read that article in the *New York Times,* but then underneath it all what is there? A lie: for we aren't a good theater; we aren't a theater that will last if we go on as we are now; we will soon run out of donations and people, the two things needed to make a theater idea work. I would like to think that when I got my name in the *New York Times* it was because of something of which I felt worthy and had earned. My tromping on makeshift stages in 28 Mississippi towns, doing an uncreative and skillfully undirected job of Idella Landy is not the sort of thing I want published in the *New York Times.* Doing *Purlie* is a scandal, but not doing it in New York, and only doing *Godot,* is hiding our dirty linen in the closet.

Last night we were called to rally to the cause—a last-moment plunge—of selling more tickets to the FST benefit. The benefit is doomed, I think, not to make any money. FST's meaning, existence, and finances must come from the South if it has any intention of being a Southern theater, which apparently it has or we would not have spent five months there. Could we not have predicted this? Some of us were against playing in NYC for reasons other than that NYC would not give two hoots about FST. I was worried that our productions were not worth doing here, for instance. I thought we were being pretentious and audacious to come tromping into NYC to perform. James and John too, I think, thought we should stay in the South because that's where our audience is and the NYC audience would only misjudge us. Despite these feelings and thoughts, we assumed that people in NYC would be interested in coming to the shows. That assumption was wrong. There are a handful of people, certainly, who are interested in promoting and encouraging us. But to sell a house of 500 seats at $4 and $10 is something else again. Now, of course, if we had drawn the country's attention to us while we were in the South, if we had built up some expectation through publicity released while we were playing, if we had taken the time to become a damn good theater, then possibly we could have arrived here like the Moscow Art Theater reappearing after 40 years, greeted with waves of enthusiasm.

Part Three

IN WHITE AMERICA
THE RIFLES OF SENORA CARRAR

GM TD *Our performances in New York attracted a lot of attention and interest; many more actors and directors applied to join the FST; we found a theater, and we organized a new company, a larger one, to undertake the 1965 tour. Tom Dent joined us in early spring. Denise and Murray stayed on as actors, Robert Cordier joined us as director and production manager, and then as artistic director after Scott Cunningham's brief stint. Robert (Big Daddy) Costley, Roscoe Orman, Joanne Forman, Betty Greenhoe, Emalyn Hawkins, Collin Lee, Mary Lovelace, Peter O'Grady, Joseph Perry, and Sally Summers made up the rest of the core of the 1965 acting company.*

By July the FST office was a mass of confusion which can only be described as astounding. Company members seemed to arrive and leave almost daily. Aside from these people, who were supposed to be paid $35 a week but often received less, the place was inundated by volunteers who came out of the blue to "help." In the space of two months a white minister and his wife from Arizona, a black clinical psychologist from Philadelphia, and a coffee shop owner and his dancer wife all came to give their vacations to FST.

The "place," the theater's home, was a dilapidated wooden structure in the Creole section of New Orleans, misnamed The Pentagon Building. The owner, a wealthy and cranky black, had offered the top floor to the FST without charge. It had been a dance hall, but had four or five rooms which were used as offices.

The FST did not take immediately in the black community. The Movement ideas, the integration, the disrespect for social convention in dress and behavior, left a bad taste in the mouths of

New Orleans blacks, who of course did not consider themselves black. Most of us lived in the French Quarter, the oldest and most legendary section of New Orleans. The temporary and integrated living (people doubled and tripled up), very much in the tradition of the Movement, was a movement in itself, and attracted considerable public notoriety.

The theater had adopted New Orleans as its home, regretfully on the part of some FST veterans (of one year), but New Orleans did not adopt the FST. It wasn't that the black community opposed the FST, it simply ignored it. There seemed to be a hope that the group, with its radical ideas, would simply fade away, or go back where it came from.

The Conscience of the King:
My Tour with the Free Southern "Circus"
The Journal of Big Daddy

Robert Costley

May 2, 1965

After 36 tiring hours, I finally reached New Orleans. I am one tired actor. Actor? The trip was uneventful, except for a few humorous incidents. Yesterday I left Louisville, Ky., about 10:30 P.M. The bus was jammed with people going to all points South, mainly Florida and Mississippi. I was sitting in the last seat in the rear. (It was the only seat vacant.) A young white woman (pregnant) and her two-year-old son followed me on. Since I got to the rear first (all of *us* are fast runners), I sat first. She asked if she could join me. I allowed her to, and we pulled out. About five miles down the road we started to converse. She said she was going to Anniston, Alabama, to be with her folks for a month. I told her I was going to New Orleans to perform with the Free Southern Theater. The first thing she said after that was "My Lord, you couldn't find anything else to do with yourself?" I explained the purpose of the group, its aims, aspirations, desires, etc. She seemed to accept it and things went along smoothly. We got to Horse Cave, Kentucky (that's the official name), about 2:15 P.M., for our lunch break. I got off, had myself a 12¢ Hershey bar and a glass of water, and returned to my seat. About 10 minutes later, my riding companion got back on with her young-un, as she called him, and asked me if I would hold him so she could fetch some "sweet milk." I agreed, and she put the child in my lap. (I never *did* know that child's name. Any time she called or scolded him it was "now young-un you stop that" or "young-un you behave yoself or Mama's gonna fan the tar outer you.") Anyhow, while she was out, the driver came through counting heads. Well! He was a new driver that got on at Horse Cave and when he saw me in that seat with this little two-year-old blond headed boy bouncing on my lap, I thought he would faint! He looked at me for about two minutes and managed to say, "Ahm one person short, is your ah, your ah-ah-*wife* in the terminal?" Before I could answer, a little white man sitting across the aisle from me said, "Driver, is you crazy? That boy ain't got no wife on this bus—that's his girl friend's baby!" I *swear* those were his exact words. I explained to the driver that the child's mother was getting it some milk, and that I was merely holding him until she returned. The driver retreated back down the aisle shaking his head as my "champion" grinned and winked his eye at me. By this time Mama was getting back on with her sweet milk. The bus pulled out and we were off to Nashville, Tennessee.

From Nashville to Birmingham, Alabama, I sat next to a little old colored lady who read her Bible and hummed spirituals for 10 hours, and at the end of that ride I damn near took the pledge. From Birmingham to New Orleans the ride was hot, dull, and tiring. Bogalusa looked like any quiet, peaceful, sleepy little town on a Sunday morning. Not a rope or burning cross in sight. At 10:00 A.M. we pulled in to New Orleans.

I have met the troupe, thirteen people in all, been assigned a role in *In White America,* and given an advance on my salary. I slept for four hours, had two rib sandwiches at a restaurant down the street from our headquarters (which is called The Pentagon Building), and read the play with the group. It is now 1:45 A.M. and I am beat.

May 3, 1965

No rehearsal of *America* today. I spent the day reading and re-reading *America,* and *Shadow of a Gunman.* Had lunch at the L.A.A. Club up the street from the theater—the menu: red beans and rice. Behind the bar: "Big Bessie," a large full-bodied woman approximately 26–27 years old who wears a large reddish wig combed down on the right side. She is loud, voracious, and full of the juices of honky tonk life.

May 4, 1965

There seems to be dissension in the ranks. I am not quite sure what or why it is. I will wait and see. Another day of idleness. No *In White America* rehearsal. I discovered Dillard University, the small Negro school on Gentilly St. Toured the campus on Murray's bike. The temp reached 88.

May 5, 1965

Took my first ride (via a free ferry) across the Big Muddy today. The bench you sit on while waiting to board the ferry carries two rusty tin signs at each end, one marked "colored" and one marked "white." I sat in the middle of the bench, I'm non-committal.

Rode through New Orleans' new downtown civic redevelopment center. The New Negro Old Folks Home on Erato and Simon Bolivar Ave. looks like a new hotel or an exclusive new high-rent apt. building. It is marvelous.

We're back to rehearsing *In White America*—great.

May 6, 1965

At 10:00 A.M. we had the first seminar on Brecht at the home of Richard Schechner, one of the three founding and producing directors of FST. The man is young (middle 20's) energetic, interesting, and brilliant. This will be a weekly occurrence, and I am eagerly looking forward to all of them.

May 8, 1965

Went to Bessie's party at the L.A.A. lounge. I was only there for five minutes when Bessie was ready to shoot one of her guests. I have never seen such big women in my life. Bessie must weigh 220. A young pretty girl came to the "party" last night, she was about 5′8″ or 5′9″, she was proportioned, she was just a "big child," and she must have weighed 250. Maybe it's due to the very high humidity, but a large percentage of N.O. women do not wear girdles. And those that do not wear them are the ones that need it most.

May 9, 1965

Mother's Day—I wonder what Frank and the [Costleys'] children did today. I miss them more and more each day. I wonder how long I can bear to be away from them.

I went out to City Park. It looks like a man-made version of a Louisiana bayou. There are 35 tennis courts here. These courts are equipped with lights for play at night. It costs you 40¢ per hour to play on the concrete courts and 50¢ per hour for the treated courts. I met, I was informed, the total Negro tennis-playing crowd today—eight men. I was told there was not a single Negro female in New Orleans who could play even a passable game of tennis.

On returning from the park I was invited into the apt. of Gilbert and Denise Moses, where I found Roscoe and Peter and had a delicious supper. Gilbert, one of the three original founders of FST, is a very intense, brilliant young man. He plays the guitar, sings in a melodious appealing voice, and reads everything on drama, art, politics, the Negro. A young man with a searching, quick, facile mind. His wife Denise has the most exquisite skin tone, with silky brown hair and laughing eyes. Her face is that of a Nile River queen. Roscoe is a handsome young man in his early twenties who is probably the most talented male member of the group. He sings (he was with Oscar Brown, Jr., on Broadway), dances like a feather, is a sensitive actor, a clever mimic, and has a good comic's sense of timing. His face has "instant charm" written all over it. Peter is a white boy from Illinois who is attending college at Tougaloo. He has the dark good looks of a young Gregory Peck, and a sincerity about him that is most refreshing. The five of us sat around and sang, told jokes, drank coffee, ate ice cream, talked about the future of FST, the strange effect of N.O. on us, and our personal feelings about FST. Being around all these young, fearless, energetic people has given me a new birth of "artistic freedom" as far as theater is concerned. I wonder if Frank and Mrs. Wofford got their Mother's Day messages and if they were surprised.

May 10, 1965

Tonight I moved in with Steve Rubin [pastor of N.O.'s First Unitarian Church] and his very charming wife Gail, their two hilarious children Josh and Jennifer, and a magnificent Basenji dog named "Jones." Steve and I must have talked for three hours on "the Movement" and a more stimulating evening I haven't had since I don't know when.

May 11, 1965

I rode Murray's bike home tonight. Five and a half miles. I got here at 10:50. I sat on the steps and smoked a cigarette because I was bushed. I couldn't get my key to work. I tried three or four times and finally it opened. I came in, washed up, got in bed, and read about 12 pages of a new magazine called *NOW*. I turned out the light, smoothed out my pillow, turned over to get comfortable, and I heard a loud explosion in front of the house. I jumped up, ran out on the sun porch (in my drawers), and there was a car all in flames parked at the curb. I didn't want to wake the Rubins so I just stood watching and wondering why the fire department wasn't right there, and lit up a Camel. After about six or seven minutes, the fire dept. arrived, and I called Steve, thinking they probably wanted him to move his car. Then I found out it was his car that was bombed. When he got outside the police informed him that his church had also been bombed. I confess—I am scared. The FBI was called.

What kind of minds are we dealing with? I am sleeping in the Rubins' children's room, which is in the front of the house. Suppose they had tossed the bomb at the house?

That's the end of sleep for this night. Steve got out his double-barreled shotgun and loaded it. And I said, "Crazy, have you got one for me?"

May 12, 1965—6:00 P.M.

I am sitting in City Park in front of the Isaac Delgado Museum of Art. This "quaint" old city of New Orleans is to me a city of lights and shadows, fears and hates. I have never felt so apprehensive or edgy in a city like this in my life. The Law says you may go and be served where you wish. But the help, the owners, and the patrons in a number of places fairly seethe with resentment. In the last three days I have put forty-seven miles on Murray's bike just seeing the city. I find the middle-class "Southern belle" to be rather dowdy, overweight, dull, and unaware. Her "fashions" are circa 1959–1962. Her Negro counterpart buys a $65 wig and neglects girdles or even a garter belt. Stockings rolled to the knee is still common on a goodly number of young ladies. I have honestly not seen more than a dozen naturally pretty women, black or white, in this city. I am told that the campus of Xavier has a bountiful supply. Well, it is time to hop on Murray's bike and ride the three and a half miles back to rehearsal. The temperature today reached 92.

May 12, 1965—1:15 A.M.

It is small wonder the Negro woman is thought of and propositioned as a prostitute by white and black men. As a rule, the taller, heavier, more amply endowed she is, the louder and shorter her apparel becomes; and the pity of it is she *swears* she is high fashion, regardless of whether the clothes fit or not.

Almost without exception, in both white and colored sections of the city, the New Orleans postman is a Negro. But in the four post offices I have visited the clerks, countermen, and foreman are 95 to 99 per cent white. You still see, on private lawns, in front of businesses downtown and in the quarter, the ebony jockey, the Mammy, and the "Nigger Jim" statues. Soft drink trucks always have a white driver, dressed in white shirt, tie, and neat dark slacks, and the "frog" in coveralls, who does the "fetchin' and carryin'." All bread trucks have white delivery men. The public works gang may have six to ten fellows on it. Most of the laborers are colored, but the "boss man" is *always* white. I have yet to see an integrated work gang. Either it is all white or all black with a white foreman.

Bob Landers, a professor of history at Tulane, spoke to us at the theater today. He stated that after the Civil War 75 to 80 per cent of all the armed forces of the U.S. were Negro soldiers. One of the last white divisions was wiped out with Custer at Little Big Horn. The "Buffalo" soldiers of the cavalry in the West were all Negroes. The troops that captured Geronimo were Negroes. Negroes were also the first soldiers to reach San Juan Hill. When T. Roosevelt's "Rough Riders" got to the top, "Joker Jones" was already there with the situation well in hand. How 'bout that. The first Negroes to join the Union forces in the Civil War came from New Orleans.

May 15, 1965

Tonight we preview our first show, Brecht's *The Rifles of Senora Carrar.* I played a fisherman, three whole lines. I was "thrown" in as a last-minute replacement for John O'Neal, who had to go to St. Louis and Jackson, Miss.

It is apparent from this first show that this company has a long way to go. 90 per cent of the actors are amateur. Emalyn does a fine job, and Murray does a superb job as the priest. Roscoe is quite good as the youngest son. But Gil, Denise, Collin, Patricia, are not with it. Steve and Gail Rubin went, and they were not impressed. I can understand it. *White America* is sort of dragging its heels. My recording [of the original cast performance in New York] arrived. The cast heard it and dismissed it as "nothing." Some of the comments were: "Gloria Foster irritates me with that down homey quality in her voice," "There isn't an actor here that can't do better!" "It sounds like a high school reading," "The whole thing sounds phoney."

I don't know why Scott is deluding these kids into thinking that they can "top" this (to me) perfect cast. If he will just unbend, be truthful about the limitations of his cast, I think we can possibly give a good show. If not we are going to look like a bunch of amateurs posturing and posing about on the stage, signifying nothing.

May 19, 1965

Saturday night I moved. Finding decent living quarters seems to be the hardest job of the Negro members of the company. The white members can live all over the city in either the colored or white sections. But "Aunt Hagar's" children do have a bit of a time finding roach-, ant-, and rat-free dwellings.

Tomorrow night we preview *Carrar* at Dillard University. Saturday we go back to Tulane and Sunday we take *Carrar* to Tougaloo College in Mississippi.

Progress Report
Free Southern Theater
Summer 1965

Operations:

1. The Repertory. After three months of rehearsal under Robert Cordier's direction FST has previewed Bertolt Brecht's *The Rifles of Senora Carrar* and Martin Duberman's *In White America* in New Orleans at Dillard, Tulane, and Xavier Universities, the Dryades YMCA, Sacred Heart Church, Guste Homes, St. Peter Claver School Auditorium, First Unitarian Church, the Jefferson Parish Harlem Gym, and at Tougaloo College in Mississippi. Public rehearsals of these two plays will continue until the last week in July. The opening of the full repertory is slated for the last week in July in New Orleans, and the opening of the tour in Jackson, Mississippi, in August. If time permits Molière's comedy, *Georges Dandin,* or *The Cuckold* will also be done. During the tour we plan to revive *Waiting for Godot.* (There has been much demand for this play among FST audiences.) Performances of *Carrar* and *In White America* have been enthusiastically received and often cheered.

2. Community Project. In conjunction with the Tulane University Summer School, the FST staff will offer a lecture series in children's creative dramatics aimed at public school teachers. Workshops in puppetry, children's drama, and improvisations will be given. Also, plans have been made for a large-scale community theater project among toured towns. Limitations of finance and personnel make a pilot project in New Orleans the only immediately viable aspect of the FST program.

3. Playwrights' and Actors' Workshop. Part of each working

week is devoted to this workshop in which new scripts are tested and evolved. Gilbert Moses provides improvisations, parts of scripts, etc., to be performed by the company. In this way, plays related to our own and our audiences' experience are evolved. This phase of the FST program is just now beginning. Moses wrote the song being used in *Carrar.*

4. Training. Speech and movement classes are held regularly in the company and are mandatory for all actors. A special seminar on modern theater has been conducted by Richard Schechner.

The Company:

The company is almost entirely professional and Equity. Although salaries are well below Equity levels (maximum $35 per wk.) an informal arrangement with Equity permits the employment of union actors at what are exploitative wage rates. Hopefully this situation can be remedied soon.

The company is more than double the size of last year's, and a significant number of hold-overs assure ensemble continuity. The object of the FST is to build an organic ensemble over the next several years. . . .

The company will leave New Orleans on August 1, and remain on tour until December 19. Two week-long vacations will be used for rest and many in the company will return to New Orleans during these off periods. Experience in past tours has shown that uninterrupted touring is too exhausting both physically and mentally. The nature of the theater is such that the tour is as wearing as it is challenging. Although there has been no violence, there is the sense—especially when traveling between towns—that one is in "enemy territory." The company will visit 21 towns in six states: Mississippi, Louisiana, Georgia, Alabama, Tennessee, and Arkansas. The company will remain in each town for about a week. Plays, workshops, and public rehearsals will be offered. A typical week's schedule might be as follows: (The touring schedule is based on the following formula: six days per town, 4 performing dates, one free day, and the sixth day reserved for travel.)

Finances:

The FST, as always, is in serious financial straits. It is wrong to say "trouble," since the theater has never had much money. Benefits, small foundation contributions, individual donations have kept the FST alive. At present there is about enough money left to keep the theater alive for three weeks.

1965

In White America
by Martin Duberman

The Rifles of Senora Carrar
by Bertolt Brecht

The Shadows of a Gunman
by Sean O'Casey
[This play was ready for performance but never opened, due to lack of funds.]

Company

John O'Neal—executive producer
Mary Lovelace—administrative assistant
Lynne Sanzabacher—publicity
Frank Crump—tour manager
†Ed Pearl—assistant
Helen Brown Schechner—assistant
Gilbert Moses—producer, actor
*Scott Cunningham—artistic director (left in April)
Robert Cordier—director, artistic director

John Cannon—actor
Robert Costley—actor
Bessie Dill—actress
†Edna Gellhorn—actress
Emalyn Hawkins—actress
Marisa Joffrey—actress
*Colin Lee—actor
Victor Lewis—actor
Murray Levy—actor
Denise Nicholas—actress
Roscoe Orman—actor
*Joe Perry—actor
Richard Schechner—actor
Trish Van devere—actress
William Zukof—stage manager
David McLaughlin—technical director
*†Mathilde Shepard—assistant stage manager
Hammett Murphy—technical assistant
Peter O'Grady—technical assistant
Willa Radin—costume mistress
Betty Greenhoe—speech instructor
†Kate Pearl—dance instructor

Apprentices

†Averna Adams
†Yvonne Johnson

Community Workshop Program

Joanne Forman—director
*†Susan Ferrer—assistant director

* Present for only a portion of the time and replaced by others on list.
† Volunteers who worked without pay.

Tour Schedule

August 1–6 —Jackson, Miss.
August 7–10 —Edwards, Miss.
August 11–14—Vicksburg, Miss.
August 15–18—Jonesboro, La.
August 19–22—McComb, Miss.
August 23–26—Bogalusa, La.

The tour was terminated after one month for lack of money.

From Big Daddy's Journal

May 21, 1965

Last night we opened with *Carrar* at Dillard. In my opinion the play still is not off the ground. I placed myself in the rear of the theater, and I had trouble hearing Gil and Emalyn. Murray and Roscoe were just great.

Coming home Willa [Radin, wardrobe mistress for the show] and Patricia got into a screaming argument about the distribution of the work load between cast and crew—it was nonsensical and sickening. We had a snack at Dumaina and Rampart, where we were joined by Dick Schechner and his fiancée, and Robert Cordier and his sister-in-law, and the conversation was a hodgepodge of backbiting, pompous arrogance, snide remarks, and self-indulgence.

I did a great scene in class today for the *America* rehearsal. Scott was ecstatic with joy and the cast gave me a round of applause, the first time this has happened since FST began. At last, they know who the pro is.

May 24, 1965

We were supposed to leave for Tougaloo, Miss. at 8:00 A.M. sharp. We didn't leave until 9:15. It was decided that since it might prove difficult or embarrassing for us to try to eat together in Mississippi we would have breakfast in the open-air coffee house at the French Market here in N.O. We had been there about 15–20 min. when our waiter told us we had "used up" our time and would have to "get off the seats." We were already late getting started so we left. Gil and Scott went to lodge a "formal protest" with the manager. This done, we finally got on our way.

The trip through northern La. and southern Miss. was hot, cramped, and uneventful. At approximately 2:15 P.M. we drove through the white archway of Tougaloo Southern Christian College. It is situated about 8–10 miles outside of Jackson. My first impression on driving on the campus was one of surprise and pleasure. I had imagined I would find buildings one step removed from log cabins with leaning outhouses for "comfort stations." Instead, I found a modern rec hall and snack bar, sturdy houses that serve as dorms, classrooms, and a library. In the very center stands The Big House. It is 150 years old and repeated paintings and whitewashings have preserved it in the classic ante-bellum fashion. There is a tree in the middle of the campus called "The Great Oak." It is reputed to be over 800 years old! I stood beneath it, and its great age and quiet dignity seemed to leap out at me. It has seen the original red man that lived on this land. It stood straight and tall while hundreds of slaves bent under the lash. It has seen thousands of seasons, been the home of millions of birds and squirrels, a carving board for lovers, and a whipping post for uppity slaves. As I stood sheltered by its great arms, in my mind's eye a panorama of days long gone rushed by me and for a few moments I could hear the sound of the lash, the singing and crying of those in bondage.

I thought the performance this evening was down. Robert said it was the greatest yet. That's his problem. The discussion period that followed, as it does each of our performances—an FST first to my knowledge—was spirited, intelligent, and illuminating.

After we had struck the set and the campus had settled down

for the night, "Matchless" [Joe Perry] and I sat on the front porch of the men's dorm in the quiet stillness of a cool Mississippi night and talked of cabbages, kings, and many wondrous things. Scott and Trish were inside watching Clark Gable and Marilyn Monroe in *The Misfits.*

May 25, 1965

At 10:00 A.M. we took a look at a farm or two "back yonder," behind the campus. We spoke for about an hour to an untutored, marvelous 60-year-old lady who told us a little bit of the old days. She was beautiful.

At 1:45 we left for N.O. We arrived at 5:45–6:00 P.M. and fell into tubs and showers, still affected deeply by Mississippi. The first two weeks of August will see FST back in Jackson for one full week.

May 25, 1965

Tonight we played *Carrar* at Xavier University—a good show. A reporter from *Time* was there. He will "live" with us for the next 2–3 weeks.

May 28, 1965

Today Scott Cunningham, Trish, and Colin left the company for good. I am sorry to see Scott go. It was because of him that I am here. We had a company meeting to try to determine the reason for Scott's hasty departure. But no matter what state we are in now the FST will go on.

June 5, 1965

Last night as we were going through a final run-through of *Carrar* in preparation for our trip to Columbus, Mississippi,

Denise suddenly became ill, with a fever and pains in her abdomen. A doctor was summoned, took her temp (103), and decided to admit her to the hospital. His tentative diagnosis was acute appendicitis. That ended the Columbus trip then and there.

June 22, 1965

We are so demoralized. For three weeks we have been receiving "partial" payment of our grand salaries. The police have been harassing us like crazy. Roscoe was busted June 19th for riding his bike the wrong way on a one-way street! He was fined $30. Joe Perry was stopped and questioned at length about why he was driving a station wagon (ours) that was not registered in his name. Robert Cordier was booked at 4:00 A.M. for being in a Negro neighborhood without identification. Lynn was stopped and questioned this A.M. because she was "seen" with this "integrated group." She was asked, "How is Mr. [Murray] Levy? He's a very fine fellow, isn't he?" She said, "Yes he is." The cop said, "My ass!" Sometimes we feel like motherless children.

July 14, 1965

Dear Sir,

Last winter the Community enjoyed your play, *Waiting for Godot,* very much. We were wondering if you could make another appearance at M. I. [Mississippi Institute] College in West Point, Miss. Please let us know what date would be OK with you in Aug.

We would enjoy having you very much.

Thank you in advance.

Yours for Freedom,
John Buffington

Dear FST,

Tonight is a very lonely night for me. I am remembering last night with you and the nights before. You really made Bogalusa come alive in the three days you were in Town.

I will never forget you fine people and I don't think the city of Bogalusa will either (speaking for the Negroes). You were different from anyone that has been to Bogalusa. We miss you and want you back.

I hope to be coming to see you Sunday. Then maybe some day you will be able to return to Bogalusa. If only for a visit.

I hope you enjoyed me as I enjoyed you. I have met many people in the Movement but none was like you.

Keep up the good work, and remember me and the people of Bogalusa, for we shall always remember you.

You are Unforgettable!

You shall live in our hearts forever.

Keep Up The Good Work
Hattie Mae

From Big Daddy's Journal

August 1, 1965

At 8:45 last night I took the Illinois Central from New Orleans to Jackson, Mississippi, as advance man on the first leg of our grueling tour. It is 1965, and I rode in a segregated coach.

I arrived in Jackson at 1:05 A.M. Little Frank Crump met me at the station and carried me out to Tougaloo College where I saw Averna Adams again and it was a delight to see this beautiful child. We sat up until 5:00 A.M. as I filled them in on "the happenings" of the last five weeks.

In White America preparations for opening night were to say the least chaotic! Our screen was delayed, we had to play outdoors instead of in, we only could get 105 chairs, we had no formal way to seat audiences, no house lights, and were inundated with children as thick as roaches. At 8:15 we had 350 people waiting to see the show, at 8:45 we hit. For the next two and a half hours we had rapt attention. It was beautiful. Our curtain call was greeted with wild applause. We could have taken 20 curtain calls. They were still applauding as the tech crew moved in to start taking apart the set. It was wonderful until a "Movement" female, Negro, pulled Emalyn Hawkins' hair, and Emalyn ran off like a wild woman and the girl and her friends went looking for her. I got the station wagon, whipped around to the back entrance of the church, pulled her inside, and sped off. So we had a "security" meeting at Tougaloo where I informed them that if I was to protect their asses they must obey me. I am not sure if it sunk in. The "day" ended at 3:00 A.M.

Last night we opened *Senora Carrar* to about 230 people. Our banner was up, our house lights were up, and it was beautiful. The show, which I detest, was fair. I think the audience dug it. But I still think it is a poor choice for Mississippi—or New York!

August 8, 1965

Today we are in Mt. Beulah, Miss. Mt. Beulah is what's left of a college set up by, I think, the American Friends Society. Tomorrow night we will do *America* here at Emmet Till Hall. All of the dorms, classrooms, and offices are named for civil rights workers who have either fallen in battle or made a lasting contribution to the movement. Mr. Crump, who made three trips here, has done little to make it easier for us. We may have to replace him. After we finish here we play three days in Vicksburg, which was our original tour stop and is only 12 miles from here. Tonight I witnessed something I had never seen. We had a torrential thunder storm with much lightning but the sun setting in the west was still a ball of range fire—an eerie, wild, and wonderful sight.

Jonesboro, La., August 16, 1965

Last night in *America* the audience really got involved. They stood in the aisles, on chairs, and on benches, and gave us six curtain calls. We had gone off stage and had to return and we sang verse after verse after verse of "Oh, Freedom." They continued singing as they marched out of the hall and then had a songfest outside for at least half an hour! It was truly beautiful.

We arrived here night before last about 10:00 P.M. We were assigned to our temporary homes, and then the shit hit the fan.

Joe, Ro-Bear, and Billy Zukof went out together in search of food. They went to "Johnson's Joy Room" and finished eating about 12:15. On their way home, about a block from the house where Joe and I were staying, BAM!! The town's two Negro policemen stopped them. They made them get out of our station wagon. Each cop had his revolver drawn and the older one also had a rifle. In about three minutes, three cars of white cops had joined them, and surrounded Joe, Ro-Bear, and Billy. The Negro cops then went into their Tom act. "Yes sir, Mr. Jim; no sir, Mr. Mac; we held them for you, Mr. Charlie." Our fellows were then taken to the station and the fun began anew.

"Whatchu doing down here, pretty boy?" (To Robert) "Zukof, eh? That's a foreign name, ain't it?" (To Billy) "Where you from, *boy*?" (To Joe).

Then they were taken separately into a room upstairs and questioned for an hour and a half about "what the FST really stood for." "How is that black pussy?" (To Robert and Billy) "How does it feel to screw a white woman, boy?" (To Joe) and on into the night.

They released them at 2:00 A.M., on foot, and then followed them in a cop car. They alerted the Klan that two nigger lovers and a nigger were loose—"so pick them up for us."

The fellows walked for a while down a lonely country road and then hit the weeds. For the next three hours they crawled, ran, stumbled through that black forest as cops and Klansmen rode up and down the highway trying to find them, with their flashlights and searchlights shining through the bushes and trees. It was three hours of abject terror.

Billy finally went into a house, used the phone, and one of the Deacons came and got them. Speaking of the Deacons, Jonesboro is their home, and last night ten of them stood guard as we performed. Tonight there were ten more.

Here in Jonesboro we found a rare jewel in the form of Bessie Dill. She looks and sings like a young Odetta. This girl is beautiful. She is joining us and I am happy.

McComb, Mississippi, August 21, 1965

This is the final night of our three-day stay here in McComb. While here I have met wonderful soul people. Mrs. "Mama" Quinn, who has been bombed out of both her home and her restaurant; Willie B. Lewis, a completely charming young lady who is a waitress at one of the local restaurants; Big Roy Lee, a mountain of contained "non-violent" energy, and many, many more. Our first performance, which was *Carrar* and held at the colored movie house on Summit Street, was a disaster. The audience was noisy, rowdy, and quite disconcerting. The last two performances of *America* were held at Rose Hill Baptist Church.

The big news in McComb, for us, anyway, was the fact that our large truck turned over while trying to avoid an accident on Highway 51, about ten miles from here. Billy Zukof was driving with Dave McLaughlin next to him. Fortunately neither one was hurt. The windshield wasn't even cracked. But our sets and most of the lights were either weakened, cracked, or broken. Our paint cans overturned, too, and spoiled a great number of our props. Tomorrow we leave for Bogalusa, La., and the Deacons will be there—again—Thank God!!

Bogalusa, La., August 22, 1965

Today we met the Bogalusa Deacons, and what a reception it was. We were met by three of them about 15–20 miles outside of town. They took us over, and brother, for the very first time on this first leg of the tour we all felt perfectly safe. One of them drove our truck, one rode as "scout," and one rode the rear guard. All of them kept their firearms beside them on the seat. After arriving in town we were taken to the CORE freedom house where we were assigned our "homes" and were taken to dinner at the home of the president of the Deacons, Mr. A. Z. Young.

Bogalusa—home of the White Citizens Council, the Klan, and the number two home of the Deacons. The Garden Spot of the south. The Crown Zellerbach Co. of San Francisco provides about 75 per cent of the work here. The plant is smack dab in the middle of town. The "Frogs" live on one side and "Mr. Charlie" lives on the other. We are playing at the Union Hall—for Negroes. This is a small airtight brick structure that seats approx. 250 people, uncomfortably. We opened with *America* and it was probably not our greatest performance, but truly our greatest audience. Dick and Helen Schechner, Tom Dent, and Margaret Hellbach came up to see us. It was hot and sticky but no one left. It was great to see Dick and Helen and Margaret. I really dig those three people. Last night we did *Carrar* to another packed house. Matt Herron photographed us. Our final show was "The Bogalusa Story." It was as great as "The Jonesboro Story." Victor and Dave really gave outstanding performances.

Joe Perry played my son, and the kid was brilliant. And Bessie and Roscoe were superb!!! That Bessie is really something!

After the show we went to our favorite club for about two hours. Then Joe and I left for New Orleans. I am flying to Buffalo to be toastmaster at a dinner for Adam Clayton Powell. Joe is going home to Atlanta. The rest of "my children" are heading for NYC to try and raise money for us.

September 27, 1965

Today the roof fell in! We are "suspending" operations for about three or four months. I feel that John O'Neal made the only decision he could make. John tries so hard, and with the help of Dick and Helen does the very best he can. I dig this young man. Ro-bear is leaving for good; another chapter closed. The rest of us must begin again. Gil and Denise, Roscoe, "Father" Murray, Victor, Emalyn, and Joanne Forman will remain to keep our "eternal flame" alive. Joe is going to NYC to study. I go home . . . to raise money and to wait again for the call to return to my real home now . . . FST.

TO: Al Lowenstein, David Rothenberg, Ethel Grossman, Carol Feinman, *et al.* [Members of the New York Committee for the FST]
FROM: John O'Neal
RE: Suspension of Operations

The production program of the FST has been suspended and several people have been released. Those remaining in New Orleans include: Gilbert Moses, Denise Nicholas, Murray Levy, Roscoe Orman, Emalyn Hawkins, Joanne Forman, Richard and Helen Brown Schechner, John O'Neal, Mary Lovelace O'Neal, and Victor Lewis. They will continue to work in workshops, concentrating on the development of ensemble-playing techniques and working with acting problems, scene work, voice and speech work, and doing part-time jobs while an all-out effort is made to acquire $45,000. If we do not meet this funding requirement either in visible assets or a guaranteed income, it's my candid opinion that it will be necessary to deal with the question of whether or not the idea of the FST will live to fruition in reality. Our experience over the past few months, I think, demonstrates that it is not wise and, I don't think, possible to try to conduct a theater without certainty of wherewithal. All plans that are made under conditions of uncertainty are finally contradicted and disrupted by our inability to fund the programs we start. Rehearsal schedules, touring schedules, administrative programs, training programs, all depend on our economic capacity to bring these programs off. Since the beginning, about two years ago, we have been behind ourselves and have never been able to relax into the development of the plans that we set down on paper. This is simply to assert that we need money to carry on a program.

FUTURE PLANS: What of the status of those people who were released? I have encouraged everyone who left here to continue to think of themselves as being related to the FST, although I have intended to make it clear that the real decision as to personnel in the future depends largely on the judgment of the person who becomes artistic director. In this way, I think, we retain their good will and their potential value as fund raisers. They all understand the central problem as being an economic one. Cordier has been told that he will not be the artistic director although we tried to keep alive the possibility that he could return at some point to direct one of our plays in the future. Robert Costley, Big Daddy, we continue to think of as a member of the company in spite of the fact that he could not afford to spend these next three months here in New Orleans because of a crisis in his family. According to our information, Joseph Perry, Bessie Dill, Robert Cordier, Marisa Joffrey, Hammett Murphy, Billy Zukof, Peter O'Grady, Corey Krasko will be in New York and will be willing to do some work for the Friends. John Cannon will be in San Francisco, Big Daddy will be in Buffalo where he'll spend most of his time engaged in fund-raising activities for the theater and could be quite helpful to you in New York City. His Buffalo address is: Robert Costley, 127 Monticello Place, Buffalo, New York, Tel: 883–1319.

GENERAL COMMENTS: These first considerations, in a real sense they're primary, have dealt with some of the business problems that were resulting from the way that we were operating. Along with this, naturally, go some problems with aesthetics. We found ourselves drifting artistically, forcing work out in a rather hackneyed fashion, coming up with clichés rather than clarity, surface slickness rather than depth, not being able to meet our repertory needs under the pressure of disrupted schedules, and even considered, for a time, trying to make paying performances. We have not made the kind of progress toward an ensemble style that we have all felt was so important to theater and have suffered from the lack of contact and communication with our chosen audience. These problems, in themselves, would not be devastating or insurmountable except that we felt ourselves becoming victims of circumstance rather than its masters. It seems too, then, that the only way we can make the kind of artistic progress we desire is to cut back to this small group and to try to build our theater with our own hands and bodies, minds and souls at its core rather than to try to live according to a fictitious blueprint that we did not choose but that was forced upon us.

October 19, 1965

Al, Ethel, Dave, and Carol,

I don't know whether you were able to pick it up from that long fumbling memo I sent up there last week or not, but things have been more chaotic than usual down here. The small group that is left is now beginning to feel comfortable with itself and is relaxing (I think!) into the task at hand—the effort of self-support and fund raising between now and January.

We're going to have a rather complex travel schedule between now and then. Richard and Helen will be arriving in New York. Dick is coming up to review the Lincoln Center opening, and Helen will concentrate on trying to lay the groundwork for communication and planning for the Lincoln Center benefit that's been offered if we do the setting-up work. That means that you and the other people in New York will have to do that. We cannot afford to bring less than $3,000 on that affair. I think we should shoot for $5,000. At any rate, the two of them will only be there for four days.

We have been the recipient of a Special Achievement Award by the New England Theater Conference. Denise will go to Boston to receive the award on the weekend of October 22–23.

Mary and I will be in St. Louis for some time during the next week for my trial on the C.O. charges. My attorneys, however, have informed me that as the result of a memorandum filed with the Justice Dept. the case is going to be dismissed. This means that I'm probably going to find it necessary to do alternative service since I will be granted the 1–O classification. This too creates problems as it threatens my relationship to the FST.

Richard, Helen, and Denise will all have returned by the time we return from St. Louis. At that time, Denise and Gilbert will be dispatched to California to organize funding support out there at the expense of Ed and Kate Pearl,* our benefactors from the West Coast. Roscoe and Victor will at the same time go to Chicago, where they will try to make a committee out of our contacts there. Murray will be working in San Francisco. He left today. One or both of these teams will return to New Orleans by the 15th of November, when Richard and I will be en route to a theater conference and symposium being sponsored by *TDR*.

That brings us to the first week of January, when we'll make the effort to assess our position, make the decision about whether we can add about four more people—preferably people we already know; they will probably include Jim Cromwell and Robert Costley and probably two women, one black and one white. We will make a concerted effort to keep the group small this time and to control the rate of growth very carefully. . . .

Since the "formal structure" of the Friends [of the FST] was established I haven't been able to quite understand exactly what the communication channels in that area have been. Because I'm

* A couple who had donated their vacation time and $5,000 to FST the previous summer.

not sure, I'm sending copies of this letter to Carol and David. From the conflicting ideas in your letters to us here, it seems that you aren't sure of where you stand either. I understand that situation well because it always is like that down here—which is perhaps the reason for your own disorientation. . . .

John O'Neal

GM *There was almost a five-month lull between the suspension of operations and the beginning of work on the next season. During that time, a crystallization of what the FST to my mind had become took place. We had built a legitimate, professional touring company—a hard enough thing to do in itself—but that company and its standards, on a dirt level, had become "white." We were no closer to the idea of our original intent than we were when we began.*

The FST had to turn itself around.

November 14, 1965

Dear John,

First of all, let me say that I am ashamed to raise money for the FST. That underneath, shame in regard to what we have been doing has repressed itself since we began to produce the trilogy: *America, Rifles,* and *Carrar.* Perhaps even before that, when Charles Cobb argued that the FST wasn't doing its job in Greenville before or after our first production of *In White America.* Ashamed and uncertain, but certain only of the importance of theater and the importance of inquiry. Shame in terms of our standards for what theater should be: they do not address themselves to our audience, nor to our times, but to some academic and white standard which we should not concern ourselves with.

We have understood politically that to become part of the political system of America is to become part of a mirage. That it would mean an acceptance of America's political system and its absorption of the black race. That it would mean the gradual taking on of power through the acquisition of wealth, for finally the capitalist system is built upon flesh and bones, upon exploitation of other people. To become part of the political structure, then, would have us exploit our own people and betray other members of the third world involved in overthrowing oppression. The Utopian idea of a capitalistic democracy finally ends its logic in an affluent society where all have property and are satisfied and can participate in the society.

There is one problem. The people who have political power at this point deny, or give little drippings to, others who have no property, no power to determine their own values and their own lives. In order for the Afro-American to make a living, he must shine shoes, shovel shit, or become a schoolteacher. He cannot do what he wants or become what he wants to become; this is obvious and complete, and present all over America, in every aspect of American society.

The existence of a third world: the black, brown, yellow men who are being oppressed by a white colonial structure all over the world makes me realize that the standards of a political system and of an art are yet to be found, to be discovered, and that our own life-blood is cut off by our being so short-sighted as to regard American and/or European values and standards as our aspirations. The oppressed are the only people who will come up with new solutions for the world, simply because new solutions are necessary in order to exist, just as only a theater whose life depends on its art will innovate, change art forms and standards.

I say that to be a theater that charges no admission is patronizing, and makes us dependent upon the white power structure for money and standards. I say that we should dare to be supported by the people we play for. I say that to worry about the level of acting and kind of play to such an extent that it stops us from doing the plays which make an immediate connection is wasting not only our time but our audience's time. I say that if we can't come up with our play, or work until we have our own play, or search as meticulously as possible for plays written by Afro-Americans and other members of the third world (Africa especially, Cuba), then we will only continue to feel dissatisfaction.

What I do think is wrong is our thinking process. Our process and our direction. The Negro problem is contained in the direction from which the Negro's life comes, that is by the definition he accepts of himself. Heretofore the direction has come from outside, defined by white America. We had thought to instill dignity into the Afro-American from within. Thought. Education. Yet as long as the Afro-American takes his direction from America, he will always be subjugated. America is white. Irrevocably. We should have known that one habit had to be replaced by another.

Rifles is a bad play, and *In White America* the second time we did it was so outdated that it made me sick. The FST decidedly has been going in the wrong directions.

What does this mean to me in terms of the FST? We should point ourselves in a different, non-integrationist direction. People in theater should think that theater is necessary—for themselves. Anyone who feels as we do about American values should be able to join us. I think we should change our name to The Third World Theater. I think we should use whatever actors we have and any from the community and play in the ghettos of New Orleans, and travel perhaps on the weekends. We should charge admission: $1.00 for adults and $.50 for children in the cities, and a somewhat lesser price in rural communities. Or I think we should stage a play that we are sure the black community will like, and afterwards start a fund-raising campaign in the black community itself, to allow us to present plays free of charge. I think we should do Frank Greenwood's play *If We Must Live,* and Doug Turner's *Day of Absence,* and possibly William Branch's *Medal for Willie,* and possibly a play of mine if it is good enough. In other words, I think we should start over.

I think we should attack the morality of the U.S. and of our audiences by doing the *Dutchman* and *Slumming*. Such puritanical views belong to the burning repression of Christianity, which is finally the most primitive and racist religion that I can think of. Once it is established that salvation and purification comes from belief in one God or through a monolithic religion, then the foundations of racism and fascism are established.

The Third World Theater should bring as much as it can out in the open and face it, or be destroyed by it. No ideology has the right to restrict thought, and I should oppose any ideology that attempts to do so, in whatever form it may exist.

In terms of fund raising here, I will continue, hoping only to point to what we have done, for we need money now to live and to work. But I will approach fund raising this time at least with a clear idea of what we should be doing when we return. I will know where I'm at.

The FST for me is dead, and I can't apologize for its compromising carcass any longer. Our experience in running a theater is instrumental in bringing this theater about—we have had actors and we ourselves have a kind of reputation. I repeat: the FST is dead for me. What we did in the past is history. Let's get our money and start a theater.

We have a culture that can be developed but we black people don't respect it: Our skin features, our hair, the dialect, the blues, and jazz . . . These are the things that have Negrified American culture, and at the same time the very things we reject. The Negrification of American literature is apparent in any new novel you pick up, and in the language that modern white hipsters use. White America adopts these things almost as quickly as we try to discard them.

But when Johnson says, "We shall overcome," that is the last straw. Although I cried on that occasion I should have realized that the pronouncement was instead a presentiment, and the beginning of a new struggle. When the government absorbs us, then the Negro revolt is won. Pressure is relieved. We are in. The struggle from then on will be orderly and through the political structure.

If there is really something unique in the black experience in America, I'm not going to destroy that by becoming part of a system that has oppressed us for centuries. It is obvious by the very fact of oppression that this system is unable to recognize the right of other human beings to live when those other human beings are different but necessary (their exploitation is necessary) for that system to continue to exist. It should be obvious that if we don't have our human rights by now this system and its standards are incapable of recognizing them, of making them ours. This country is only capable of absorbing, never of change. But to whom do we turn for standards? I say that there are a group of Afro-Americans, whites, and Africans who should come together in order to discover those systems and standards of art and values which really guarantee freedom, self-determination, and the right to inquire and dissent.

The search for roots leads us, then, back to Africa.

Do I now believe in a propaganda theater? Yes. But let future generations judge that. For me, art is protest.

Respectfully, ah is yo' black friend,
Gil

GM
RS *We went into a fantastic period of disintegration and soul-searching. During February and March 1966, anyone who predicted the theater would last longer than a week was a fool. The central conflict was the black-white thing, but there were personal and organizational conflicts too. But the central thing was the desire of key people, the artists, particularly Gil Moses, to make the theater black, to really push it. It became a personal thing because Gil expressed his desire to change the theater in terms of demands for personal control. Other key people in the theater were not willing to surrender their voices without a fight.*

TD *My reaction to all this was both a despair and a hopelessness and fatal fascination. There were several things going on:*

1) Gilbert and Denise wanted a black theater pure and simple, and felt the only way they could get it was to take over.

2) There were whites in the theater structure who didn't know what Gil meant, who couldn't conceive of an FST without them. During the summer of 1965 there was a white chick working with us who, after considerable argument on my part about the limited effectiveness of whites in the black community, told me, "Tom, the FST is not a Negro theater." I said, "Oh, but it is, it can't be anything else." By early 1966 she had left, and all who believed as she did had stepped or been forced out.

3) There were whites in the theater, like Schechner, Rhoda Dreyfus and Margaret Hellbach of the Board, and Murray Levy and Eric Lewis of the company, who agreed that the theater should be primarily black but who wanted in, if only in advisory roles. These were also the whites who had helped the most throughout the theater's existence in New Orleans.

We dove into an excruciating series of almost nightly meetings. We stretched out on the floor of Schechner's apartment, or Rhoda Dreyfus's, or Gil's, and we argued. During those few weeks, with the false gaiety of Mardi Gras all around us, the talks consumed all our energy, all our thoughts, and possibly each person's nightly dreams.

We were probing not only the role of FST but far larger territory, the unpleasant realities of race in America. We were bringing into consciousness attitudes about race which had never really been talked out between us, never been faced—by the whites because even as "liberals" they had never been challenged in this way; by the blacks because they had never forced the confrontation, had never accepted the responsibility of the protagonist.

Toward the end of the discussions John O'Neal learned that he'd won his 1–O classification, and would have to leave the theater to serve out his "sentence." According to federal law, he had to be uprooted from wherever he was living and whatever he was doing to work for two years at a job which would be "picked" from a list offered him by his Selective Service Board. The board offered two choices, both janitorial positions in Chicago hospitals.

February 15, 1966

Gilbert, Richard, and others on the board—

On the black-white question: As you all must have heard me say at one time or another I think that "black" and "white" are dysfunctional categories. It seems to me that if black and white appear as premises in an argument that purports to analysis, then black and white must inevitably find the conclusion. If such a position be followed, it seems to me that the only successful synthesis of the premises would be in a blended gray. Or as one of my esteemed colleagues once said, "The problems won't be solved until we all (he was white and interestingly enough also blind) have a nice genetic tan."

The alternatives to the blended or miscegenationary point of view are, of course, the Klan types or super-Americanism or white American nationalism, if you please; on our side is the familiar Black Nationalism. All these alternatives impress me as blind alleys. Arguments regarding the race question have virtually no relevance, it seems to me, concerning the present situation of our theater. Given the current circumstances a Black Theater would not be the FST. It would contradict the values of those people who are the theater; it would not issue from the dynamic of the group relating to itself or from the group or any individuals in the group and their relationship to the community; it would not satisfy the aim of the theater to be a liberating influence on the people who participate in the experience of the theater; it would be a move away from the position of meaningful inquiry toward the propagation of what appears to me as a fallacious position.

To be sure, those people who operate the theater must be people who can trust and respect each other. I don't know whether or not the possibility for that has been too seriously jeopardized for realization. If it seems that the decision to be made is whether to have a Black Theater or no theater at all then I would have to submit the following proposal: Let all the debts of the Free Southern Theater be liquidated by the current assets, put the corporation itself in escrow, and turn over the current balance of funds to Gilbert, Denise, and Roscoe to make whatever kind of theater they think is necessary. The only condition being that they not be permitted to use the name.

I am stopping here. I am beginning to think that it would be much better for me to come down since I have expressed myself so poorly and because it is difficult to conceive of this situation which could represent the end of the Free Southern Theater.

John

March 1967

Dear John,

So the dialogue goes on and may finalize itself in my resignation . . .

I think Richard and I want two kinds of theater, and I don't know whether my being can include both of them. I don't see any reason for a professional theater here. I see reason only for: (1) a theater in which the community participates, (2) one which throws insight—light—upon the society, and (3) one which does new plays.

It is possible for a bi-racial theater to throw light upon the society, but not without side consequences. The theater that reaches the black community should deal with the people in that community. I think the FST faces a more complicated problem than college analysis can deal with—that is, the old libertine black and white together, doing plays of social consequence.

There is a culture existing in the black community which ignores white people—and this is the culture the FST should tap and put on stage. Why should the FST put white actresses on the stage when the same thing is done on TV, in films, and in every other theater in the U.S.? It must be understood that the aspirations toward white lines of beauty are real in the black community, and not simply something to be talked about or fascinated by.

Before that theater is built which uses white and black actors indiscriminately, a theater for that black community is necessary. I'm not saying that the FST should not use white actors or actresses, but I am saying that they should be used when we have a play that we want to do that requires them, instead of having to do a play using white actors because they are part of the FST. Nor am I saying that whites shouldn't work with the FST—they should work only in key positions, and then only long enough to train black people to do the job. . . .

The pride from the FST will issue from the fact that it creates new plays, that it makes black audiences laugh and cry, and that it is predominantly black run. That is a theater for the black people established by black people—and not a white liberal idea established for the good of the black people.

I will ask Murray and Victor to stay, in special positions, and ask Helen to work with us, but not yet as a member of the company. Robert Costley cannot join us until May.

Denise, Roscoe, Murray, and I need to work awhile with these ideas in the back of our heads, until we can actually formulate the needs of the theater. It is a slow process of theater building and audience building.

I don't want to waste my time this year with a whole lot of liberal malarky. Action is what counts. And we have to stop the bullshit. . . .

I'm not really sure whether Dick and I can get along. I frankly would hate to be without him.

I am not demanding a black theater, only a theater that is run with "black consciousness," and you can't have that theater unless you have black people. . . .

Otherwise, we show we want a theater, but are not willing to take the time to build one.

I have special problems because I'm not sure whether I will be here next year, but before I leave, I will make certain that there are black people in the community left with something, who will perhaps be able to do some kind of theater, simply because they have had experience with the FST.

Gilbert

Dear John and Mary,

I am in my usual dispare (dispair?)—any way you want to spell it is alright with me cause I don't give a shit anymore.

Gilbert and Denise are away for a few days and you two are away for a few years and my tooth has been missing for at least a decade (the tooth in my dream that is). Chances are that if I don't go crazy myself I'm gonna drive everyone around me to the nut house.

New York gets more and more loathsome the longer you stay there. Maby that is why I'm such an emotional cripple, I was there for 28 years.

I have nothing to say about that monster called FST so stop nagging me about it. I don't know what to do about anything. Please dear friends give me some advice.

The truth is that I love Gil and Denise more than is healthy. Not sexually, cause I could deal with that O.K., but in a much more profound way. I do my very best work when they are here, but without them I fall apart and can do nothing except go to pieces. I think that I could work with you two on an equally great level but what's the use, you're 1300 miles away, in the Bronx no less. I shouldn't trouble you with my problems cause you got enough of your own, but I have not been able to write to anyone about the pain I'm in and you know from experience that I'm not one to keep it to myself.

I may kill S——— one of these days. He is such a clever, sly motherfucker and needs a bullet in his brain to clean it out.

Murray

Dear John and Mary,

Yesterday's letter is in part now obsolete. Actually, today things are looking up. Denise will be back tomorrow and we resume rehearsals Monday night on Gilbert's play and the two plays by Alice Childress. Tonight we are all off to Xavier to see their production of *Raisin in the Sun,* and perhaps pick up some people there to work in the workshops. Roscoe is beginning acting workshops at the YMCA until we get our own building. He may even continue to have a workshop a week there after we get our own place. Roscoe says hello. We played Monopoly last night and I won—first time I ever won. I had hotels on Boardwalk and Park Place and Tom landed on Boardwalk to my delight.

Gilbert is not sure when he will return, except that it won't be right away. He needs some time to straighten himself out. John, I find it very hard to understand why you have such hostility toward Gil. He suffers a great deal and really is not interested in power in any way that would stop anybody else's creativity. Brecht was a dictator in his theater—ask George about it sometime. . . .

My hope is that if we do our jobs well, people in the community will take over the FST by the end of the year and kick us outsiders out. That way, the black theater that I hope for will emerge organically and not be imposed. We shall see. . . .

Murray

TD *John came back to New Orleans for a day or two. He and I (I was by now formally involved) wrote an agreement which Schechner and Moses, the main antagonists, accepted. Basically it stipulated: Schechner would resign as chairman of the board, to be replaced by me. Moses would be artistic director with power to hire and fire; we would look for a building to house the theater in a "hard-core" black area of New Orleans; community workshops would be offered in drama and writing to further cement our relationships in New Orleans; we would create space for a library and Afro-American information center in our building; Stanley Taylor, who acted with us in '64, would become general manager. Though Murray Levy and Eric Lewis remained, it was understood that the company would move toward an all-black group. We decided to do Gil Moses' new play,* Roots, *and poetry developed in our company writing workshop begun in the fall of 1965.*

In a few days Gil Moses was gone, by himself, never to return. Roscoe Orman replaced him as artistic director, and slowly, the company began to unify and move toward artistic objectives.

March 28, 1966

Dear John,

Long overdue, desperately long overdue, the LETTER. Something in me prevented me from writing; sent me off on endless other tasks. But now I am able to write. Gil is gone; you are gone; I am gone; the FST is in other hands, for better or worse. I think better, or, more precisely, for a kind of "worse" other than our own worse. Gil is in a terrific bag. He's gone again, perhaps not to return, perhaps to return tomorrow.

The theater? What of the theater? But can I speak of the FST and not speak of the nuts—all of us—who made it, unmade it, made it again, and keep tampering with it like it was some imperfect machine? The little distance I have makes me see what for me is wrong with that machine; though I think I have learned the good sense not to tamper any more. But that not tampering has even been amusing: because Murray will not believe that I won't tamper; a divorce where the unmarried still believes that domestic duties will be performed. They won't. Someone else will have to diaper the baby, wash the dishes, and disrupt the home. For me the FST should be (how horrible that moral "should" reads!) an experimental theater: its art forms should be as audacious as its social setting. But the FST is just another little theater, black instead of white or taffy or brown or what-have-you. Another little theater looking for the usual kind of play: what will *our* audience like/dislike enough to like? But no artistic audacity. No experimentation with forms. And as a little theater the FST is not particularly successful: we do not really produce many plays; rehearsals are scattered, disrupted. Terrific energy is put in and not much comes out. And one is *proud* when men act their age. (Rhoda comes to my class, and during the break she is very "happy" that "they" have "acted like they should" during the past week. It's a combination patronizing/bragging that indicates something about the personnel in the theater: no men, but little boys and girls.) The pattern is so strong that one is ready to shout Hurrah! and send telegrams when Murray is sane for forty-eight hours. But the theater must be more than a kiddie-cage, mustn't it?

I'm bitter, but I don't even know why. I don't feel cheated, though I am very tired and very glad to be writing and no longer enmeshed in the business of the theater: that business was like a Dickens novel, always busily moving about, but rarely getting anywhere. Everyone is so indulgent. That's the real heritage of race in this whole damned business. Everyone is afraid of offending everyone else: so the offenses become personal, not professional, and the head-beating is done in the name of art or ideology or anything abstract enough to run off one's back. Black and white are thrown around like stones. But they are soft stones, because the real issues in the FST are elsewhere. Tom Dent, for whom I have respect, argues that artists must find their own way. Sure, but they must be artists. And I don't see any artists in the FST. An artist—a LeRoi Jones—has to be proven; he cannot be proclaimed. The FST is self-proclaimed all the way down the line; there is the danger of being sucked up by our own Madison Avenue publicity. "Theater for those who have no theater," "black theater for black audiences," "get into the community." We have endless slogans, and few workshops; a theater full of writers who write very little; actors who do not act much; a theater without performers. And community contact? It took Roscoe to start a workshop—and he never theorizes in public.

Murray has become a propagandist of the worst sort: he is Gilbert's apologist, phoning me several times a week to check on what I'm doing for the FST, like a press agent keeping in touch with his contacts. Disgusting. I haven't seen Denise, but I assume she's functioning. And Roscoe too, I assume he's functioning. Eric Lewis seems OK, though I don't know him well enough to make any comment. And Victor, intelligent as he is, is lost: what the hell is he doing here? He doesn't know. Opening dialogues, relating: that's his slogan. I go along with it all: every slogan is fine; and I'm very weary of it all. I don't trust slogans. I don't trust the abilities of those involved. I am not sure that they can get the ship out of its dock, and if they do get it out whether the ship will float. I trust you, but you're very far away.

I certainly don't trust me. I finked out, and I'd fink out again. The only thing I want to do in the theater is to write criticism, try to write plays, occasionally direct. The FST can offer me none of these things and deep down I'm no altruist willing to offer things out of love. I can't even offer love out of love, so how can I offer duties out of love? Maybe someday, not soon . . .

I don't know what I think about the future of the FST. I think new people must be brought in. But at the same time I don't care. The sense I do have is not to meddle in that to which I won't devote my full self. And maybe if those left will operate by themselves they'll find a *modus operandi* for what they're doing. They may muddle themselves toward something real. Certainly you can't direct them from your isolation in New York and I can't from my inner isolation here and Gil can't from his eternal isolation. Maybe that was the starting trouble: leaders who could not lead. Maybe now, after those leaderless leaders have vanished, those we so badly led will be able to lead themselves. Maybe. I doubt it. . . .

Richard

Part Four
DESIRE

TD *The FST was broke, the three original producing directors were gone, and through the remaining members' insistence on becoming a black theater we were losing all the support we had built.*

Then a miracle happened. We received a gift of $10,000—the largest sum from any individual ever to be given to the FST—and we still don't know who gave it.

We found our building. It was an old supermarket that had been flooded out in the horrible hurricane of September 1965. The supermarket was located in what was generally considered the worst and most dangerous black ghetto of New Orleans, Desire.

Thus began a new departure, a new direction. Thus began our romance with the ghetto of Desire.

May 27, 1966

Dear John and Mary,

Well, chillin—here I be, one mo time. But this time I'm moanin low and this old heart is troubled and heavy laden.

I am not really opposed to a *complete* black takeover as far as the administrative side of the picture is concerned. What *does* trouble me is carrying this policy straight down the line in *all* departments and right into the core of the Black Nationalist movement. There was an Afro-American Conference here approx. 3–4 weeks ago and FST participated—but NO WHITES not even Murray were invited. Now, we are preparing to go to Tuskegee, Ala, for another "Festival" and we have to "inquire" as to whether Murray (who is directing *Roots* and *An Evening of Black Poetry*) will be *allowed* to come along!!! Maby I am too old for FST. But I was under the impression that we were engaged in a free theater, *not* a political crusade. Maby FST as *I* knew it and understood it, *has* outlived or outgrown its usefulness. Admittedly I *was* disturbed last summer with the inclusion of a number of incompetent white memebers, but regardless of my feelings on that score, I was proud and happy to be working (at last) in a theatrical experience that gave free expression to all of its members regardless of their ethnic backgrounds. I imagine one of the main reasons for my disenchantment is the infiltration into our midsts of certain people who are for the most part power hungry opportunists (my spelling is LOUSY).

Working in the Desire area does have its intrisect value I *suppose,* and the fact that we are starting a library and information center on Negro/African History I suppose is uplifting—to us!! (The FST personell) But I can see our building fast becoming a 2nd or 3rd rate *neighborhood house* and less and less a *theater.* We have had more dam trouble (nothing major) with these, quote, beautiful black *deprived* children in *four months,* than in the whole 3 or 4 years existence of FST. I honestly do believe that they could give less then a dam if they never saw a *play* there, but the building is one more avenue of escape and a place to go to raise hell and meet the oposite sex. They run all through the building while we're having rehearsals and workshops, break windows, throw stones and *glass* into the building, play the bongos (if we leave them out) get surly when they are asked to leave and intimidate youngsters who are not from the immediate 4–6 block area when they come over for a workshop or a meeting. The dam building is intensely hot, no air conditioning, no fans and we *must* keep all the doors *locked* while we are there to keep from being inundated by the "populace." We have *no windows* at all—because it is too dangerous!! So all of the window pains have been knocked out and replaced by *boards!!*

This is going to be a long hot summer for me in more than one way—believe me son.

Maby I dont *fully* understand what is *really* going on or maby I have been around to long to become *enchanted* with crusading on the *grand scale*. What ever the reason, the old man is *most* unhappy.

[Big Daddy]

June 8, 1966

Dear Tom,

. . . you must begin to think in terms of letting the work of the company support the theater financially. Philanthropy can be expected to help only as long as the receiving group is spreading sweetness and light. In my own mind this also has quite a lot to do with integrity. If there is no relationship between what you do for money and what you do for yourself, either you lose respect for the money you spend because of the hassle involved in getting it; or you lose respect for the value of what you're doing, or both. I think that this is unfortunate, no, more than that I think that it's bad. The fact is, however, that we live in a society whose chief values are tied up to currency. We are victims.

I guess the simplest way of saying what I'm trying to say is that the FST should do as much as it can toward becoming self-sufficient. Until it is self-sufficient, it will be able to do or say no more than those who control the funding sources will permit it to say. Regardless of Blackism, Whiteism, or anything else. . . .

John

1966

An Evening of African and Afro-American Poetry
compiled by the Company

Roots
by Gilbert Moses

I Speak of Africa (a one-act play)
by William Plomer

Does Man Help Man?
by Bertolt Brecht

Company
Tom Dent—acting producer
Robert Costley—actor, director (*Roots*)
Sam Hill—actor
Murray Levy—actor, director (*Poetry, Man, I Speak*)
Detton Lieuteau—actress
Denise Nicholas—actress
Roscoe Orman—actor, director
Eric Lewis—technical director
Stanley Taylor—business manager
Marge Jennings—administrative assistant

Apprentices—Ollie Smith
Gilbert Matthews
Sam Hill

Community Workshop Program (May–August 1966)
Acting Workshop—Robert Costley
Roscoe Orman
Creative Writing and Black Literature—Tom Dent

Tour Schedule

July 9	—New Orleans (previews)
July 11–14	—Dillard University, New Orleans, La.
July 15–21	—Spelman College, Atlanta, Ga.
July 24–27	—Tuskegee Institute, Tuskegee, Ala.
July 28–30	—Selma, Ala.

July 31–August 17	—New Orleans, La.
August 18–21	—Hattiesburg, Miss.
August 22–25	—Laurel, Miss.
August 26–29	—McComb, Miss.
August 30–September 2	—Bogalusa, La.
September 3–5	—Jonesboro, La.
September 9–13	—New Orleans, La.
September 15	—Greenwood, Miss.
September 16	—Grenada, Miss.
September 17	—Sunflower, Miss.
September 18–21	—Kilmachael, Miss.
September 26–29	—Natchez, Miss.

June 13, 1966

Dear Denise,

. . . The company is now on the verge of psychic disintegration, because of the smoldering conflict over the course of the theater which has now broken into open flame. We must come to some resolution very quickly, or just about all will be lost.

The effect now is like a writer who can never complete a first draft because something in him is perpetually dissatisfied with it, thus he is always ripping it out of the typewriter and tearing it up. But I think we have the beginnings of a program now; because I believe we must do productions *first,* and to make them worthwhile we must at some point go along with our first draft although it isn't everything we want it to be.

First of all, if we are going to be a theater, and I have always been under the impression that that is what we are, we *must* do productions. We can talk about workshops, talent shows, library, information center, children's story sessions until doomsday, but as far as I am concerned unless the theater produces plays it simply is not a theater. Plays have a value in themselves, if, for us, they deal challengingly with the reality of the black man in America. Plays then constitute a method by which an audience is forced to face up to a reality about itself, and if a play is good, then it illustrates before an audience a type of truth which cannot be stated as well any other way. I think we have a tendency to too easily disparage the accomplishments of the touring theater of the last two years; even a play like *In White America,* though we can do better, has extraordinary educational value for black (or white) audiences.

I think a specific point of discouragement to me in your statements about the theater is a feeling I discern on your part of lack of respect for your art as an actress. I get the feeling you are really not interested in theater or the discipline and labor it takes to perform well as an actress. This is not to say that you cannot do it, I think some of your performances have been brilliant; but it is to say I do not think you are *interested* in it. I think you are interested in other things which you feel theater should do because you, at this moment, want the theater to do these things.

But I feel that if one of the prime purposes of the theater is to develop both an audience and a growing fund of creative talent in the South we must respect and develop our art, for this is the only thing that will possibly inspire and interest unexposed youth to do likewise. To develop virile theater in communities, including Desire, we must ourselves offer virile theater, to develop young writers we must write, and above all, and I say above all because I think it gets lost in these discussions of community theater, we must do what we do well. The spawn of shoddy art will be shoddy art. But to do productions and to do them well is to plant the germ of an idea.

To me this whole business about community theater or spontaneous theater or group dynamic theater results from confusion about what can be done through artistic form. In the first place, communities do not do theater, individuals do. Some individual must first write the play, which means subjecting an idea to the distillation of form, and that play represents his own vision. There is no such thing as community vision, or committee vision, or group dynamic vision. And for the writer or artist to have vision means that he sees and states the unconscious truths of a community, he focuses his spotlight on what the community lives by but does not say it lives by. This means that the artist with vision is always *ahead* of the community, therefore controversial because he has exposed the conflict between subliminal truth and surface reality. It is only later, when some of the prophet's ideas have been accepted into the hum-drum of everyday life, that *he* becomes accepted. . . .

I think there are considerable illusions about the degree of acceptance of racial reality theater will achieve in the black communities of the South, or anywhere else, because too many people are not facing those truths. This points up the essential fallacy of an all-black theater; an all-black theater could conceivably perpetrate all the ideas of Booker T. Washington or Moishe Tshombe, or do any of the other Broadwayish productions that Negro colleges have done—with an all-black cast. The value of any art is always *what it says and how it is said;* the race of who says it only takes on importance in relation to the former. Everybody wants to swing a bat but nobody wants to watch the ball.

But to get back to the relationship between the community and the theater, we relate first of all as art to audience. And then, if this is the planting of a seed, to offer workshops is go a little further and water the ground over those seeds because some of them might sprout. The thing is to take an individual and encourage him both by direct suggestions and the inspiration of, hopefully, what we do. And this is important because in the black communities the opportunity for such encouragement has never existed to the extent we can, or could, offer. And we could go a little further and do workshop productions which give the participant a feeling of completion for his efforts. But to me there is a sense of priority and development here: our own FST productions should create a community regenerative force which can be cultivated in workshops; finally the full circle is completed when the workshops produce plays of their own and then people who replace us.

But we must have this basic structure of performances, and the establishment of a relationship to the community through performance before the cultivation of community talent can really begin. Aside from shortage of personnel, the workshops are not as fecund as they should be because we ourselves aren't doing anything. Who wants to come to workshops at a theater that doesn't, or doesn't know if it wants to, put on a show? . . .

I sense a longing for panacea: everything must happen right now without our doing any work. It is this constant indecision and a lack of confidence in any program we undertake that has created a situation where we have done three or four performances in five months.

And it is not true that we don't have a program because we do, and it *can* work if we try to make it work. I feel what the company must do now is go through with the first draft—of course it isn't everything we want it to be—because until we do that we cannot make the things happen that we, or at least I, want to see happen. . . .

A Board meeting is set up for Monday night which all company members are invited to. If you do not agree with what I have outlined I hope you can draw up a proposal for the company to present to the Board at that meeting. I will do the same. Maybe then we can get all this distasteful business taken care of.

Tom Dent

TD *In the midst of our incessant internal warfare, we finally received that grant from the Rockefeller Foundation. It insured our financial survival for the balance of the summer.*

June 18, 1966

Dear John,

. . . When you talked with Big Daddy last week I guess he told you we are in another crisis. I don't see how much longer this can go on or how to summarize to you exactly *what* is going on. It is not really between Denise and myself; the entire company is now in a running series of company meetings which resemble the constitutional convention of 1785—everyone suddenly feels the need for theory and policy. Meanwhile the shows we had begun are ignored, left hanging on the vine just at the point where we should be doing previews.

The basic problem, to *try* to state it, is that no one is able, or no one is willing, to accept enough company authority to make a show work. . . . We desperately need new personnel, two more actresses, at least one, a community workshop director (your warning that the actors could not act *and* run a workshop program has proved true), and a technical director who is Negro, relatively stable, and competent. I almost feel now that the only possibility for a fruitful summer would be to abandon what we are doing now or trying to do and get those people. You understand what I mean when I say that the Free Southern Theater is built, and always has been built, on friends, lovers, and wives, and in a situation like that no one can get anything done. We suffer from a type of hemophilia caused by excessive incest, and if no new blood comes into this thing soon it's just gonna die.

A Board meeting with all company members is scheduled for Monday night. Rhoda and Margaret are interested and alarmed, Oretha and Upton have taken an active interest. I talked with Richard after he returned from New York, it was a good talk, but a lot of his statements about the "Villagy" approach to art which he made during the time of his conflicts with Gilbert I think now are true. I would like to see the company buckle down and try to carry through the present program: the poetry, *Roots,* and get *Blood Knot* into rehearsal. But there is now on the part of Denise and Roscoe a desire for a sort of company administration by consensus, which means before you can spend ten cents you have to spend three hours arguing about it in company meeting. If we could just get through *this* season and then reorganize, after I am gone, then I would be happy.

I imagine I sound like a raving maniac, but I really am tired of it, John, not so much bitter as I was earlier in the week, but I feel sort of a dull hopelessness now because whatever "decisions" come out of this reorganization will surely be reorganized by company meeting three or four weeks from now when someone gets unhappy with the distribution of power. We *need* a dictator in the worst way, someone who actually has the power to hire and fire and to carry through a policy. But that person is not here now, no one trusts anyone here enough to give that sort of power, so you see where we are. Murray is very up tight and has been for a long time, the company meetings are full of hostility though sprinkled with a forgiving humor, everyone who doesn't like someone is telling them that in these meetings, which have been going on since the day after the CBS show Wednesday the 8th when Denise submitted half a resignation letter. And if Denise leaves we ain't got no theater since she is our only actress.

The CBS show [a "Look Up and Live" documentary on six regional theaters, in which the FST participated] went very well, the Alabama shows went well enough, we have more bread than we ever did—still your letter means nothing because in the present situation we cannot plan *anything* but more meetings; my proposal means nothing, to schedule a tour means nothing, to even schedule preview performances in New Orleans means nothing, and the building, despite the work done on it, is not ready. What is depressing is we are on the verge of something, but we simply cannot do it the old way with the old people. This is what I see.

I don't know that you should come down now, I don't know that it would do any good. This problem that I see would not be solved by that. But I feel now that the Board is the only possible organ that can save this thing from a laconic, never get past one show a month rut, and maybe we can get the Board to act and make some decision Monday night.

Right now I am hoping some plays can come out of the writing workshop, that for the remainder of the summer we can accomplish something, and then I think I will have to leave. I do not want to sound terribly hopeless or pessimistic, but this is the way I feel now.

Tom

June 28, 1966

Dear Roscoe and Murray,

My head is about to blow open with everything. You people are very frustrating. I wait every week to hear the news that you've split up because you were either unable or unwilling to love and learn each other and already fear that you have lost faith in the idea that people's lives can be influenced by the theater. . . .

Keep the theater alive so that hope can continue here that one day I too can come back home. . . .

John

July 1, 1966

Dear Tom,

. . . I agree 100% with you [a reaction to Dent's letter to Denise Nicholas]: the trouble with FST has been the confusion between personal hangups and theater. There has been an alternating current in which the theater is meant to solve personal problems; and vice-versa: when things "feel sweet," then the theater should "take care of itself." You're right when you say this won't work. Even more, this kind of thinking is avoiding the issues the theater can and should deal with and a by-product of this is that people get more and more hung up.

Once all of us in the theater recognize:

That because theater can't solve *all* problems facing man in-the-South doesn't mean the theater is shit;

That because race hangs us up, it stops us;

That talk is a substitute for art, it is better than art because talk doesn't fail, it is not put to any test.

Once we recognize that the easy formulas—the ones we think by too often—are *untrue,* then maybe we can begin formulating some *operative* things. I always sound like a fink (white and old), but fink I am then, BUT:

1. A group activity takes organization and structure;
2. Structure means leadership;
3. Leadership means "democracy" can be used only at certain points—the democratic system is to "follow the leader(s)," no matter how un-Utopian that sounds;
4. Art involves, as you say, the hard work of individuals *who give up their right* to say this or that immediately *in exchange for* saying it in their art;
5. The FST is a theater, and its political effects are just that, *effects*—something that happens after, not something to be done for its own sake;
6. To be a theater means to submit to some discipline;
7. To solve the problems of being a theatre is to do something very important in the community:
    A. Showing art, and that art can be discussed and criticized and reacted to by the community;
    B. Being a living thing, the presence of which *in itself* is something this community, white and black, desperately needs.

I am sick of being thrown into the black/white bag only because I see it as an avoidance of any direct confrontation. When people want to deal with *me,* I'm usually willing to deal with them; when they want to have an abstract discussion, I invite them to class. The FST has had too much of the atmosphere of a class, where abstractions are dealt with, discussed, "resolved," but where nothing is done. I feel that the real world has eluded the theater, for all the talk about living in that world. After all Murray's revolution (and possibly Denise's) came after *reading*

Malcolm's autobiography. All well and good, except that Murray and Denise had been *living here* for two years! If the living had been authentic, Malcolm would have seemed tame. At that, they read the book out of context: the direct context of their participating life in this bitch of a city.

Those are some of the reasons I get tired of the theater. Not of the theater-as-it-could-be, but the theater as it is: the children in it. So I agree with your words, agree more than I can express. Because artistically this theater has to get off the pot.

As for your one-year plan, I think as an outline it's O.K. I would like the thing to be flexible, however. If we have the money we should have a one-year program, all year. If not, no. I think we can get foundation money and some government money (arts endowment). I agree that we need a clean sweep: a new beginning. We're too ingrown. Only you and Stanley, if you can work together, can provide for that new birth. It means getting rid of the people because they can't cross the Jordan River. And getting new people who can. The history of personal hangups over the past two years has accumulated too many memories for the company to really be efficient and artistic as now constituted. A new company after October seems to me the only rational solution.

Richard

TD *When* The Ghetto of Desire *was filmed by CBS for the "Look Up and Live" program, technicians from CBS's New Orleans affiliate assisted. One of these men, we believe, sent copies of the script to the mayor and the chief of police. Soon after, members of our Board of Directors began to receive intimidating registered letters from the Housing Authority. When officials discovered we weren't easily put down, the situation erupted into open war. The crisis over the show unified us, brought us more tightly together than we had been for a long time.*

A Section of the Television Script for *The Ghetto of Desire*

Thomas C. Dent

You think about the dimensions of the Desire Project in the lazy, tropical city of New Orleans. On the river side of the dull, reddish-brown buildings is the Florida Avenue canal, the stench from which everyone can smell as soon as the weather becomes warm. You cross the canal over a thin bridge at Louisa Street, the only junction between Project traffic and the main arteries of the city. Since the bridge is small and heavy traffic must cross it, it is usually jammed, especially now at 5:00.

Parallel to the canal is a railroad complex of four tracks. The city of New Orleans has never required the railroad which uses these tracks to reroute, thus traffic may be brought to a standstill any time of day or night while the train lumbers across at a snail's pace. Day and night residents of the Desire area hear the bark of the train horn, the horn of inconvenience.

Other sides of the Project are bounded by extremely dense brush, a smaller ditch, and, toward the center of the city, an even larger complex of railroad tracks.

The streets in the Desire area are full of holes. There is only one playground, poorly lighted and poorly supervised. There is no recreation center, no swimming pool—and many, many children. At night there are very few street lights.

There are few jobs for the dark-skinned citizens of Desire. Many mothers work as domestics for the traditional five dollars a day plus carfare. Many of the families are on welfare, never an adequate subsistence. And all of the families remember the flood which struck fiercely at every home after Hurricane Betsy, destroying what little each family owned.

You think about the mystery of a city where it is good to be white, and if not white at least light. Where people who by God's authority of creation were born black sit voluntarily on the back of the bus; where there is "good" hair and "bad" hair and a rush on the market for wigs, where it is admirable, if you're not born white, to at least imitate white people, where city officials talk glowingly of "progress" but the bark of a train horn can be the final authority over birth and death because the train horn dictates how quickly one can get to a hospital.

You wonder a bit more about why people in an area with so little owned and so much to fight for have no effective political organization of their own, no voice which speaks for the needs of the people, no consistent, overt protest against the fact that they are forgotten by the city of New Orleans.

July 1, 1966

Thomas C. Dent
President Board of Directors
Free Southern Theater
2632 Louisa Street
New Orleans, Louisiana

Dear Mr. Dent:

It has come to the Authority's attention that a script entitled "Ghetto of Desire" is to be presented nationally on the program, "Look Up and Live" by CBS on August 7, 1966—WWL of New Orleans and possibly certain other local stations excepted. It is our understanding that the script was filmed by WWL for CBS at the Free Southern Theater Playhouse, 2632 Louisa Street, the script, plus a discussion period that followed its staging, the product of members of the Free Southern Theater.

I contacted Mrs. Leonard Dreyfus, a member of the Board of Directors of the Theater, and she kindly agreed to a conference, which took place at my office on June 30. After considerable discussion it was agreed that I and other representatives of the Authority should present our views on this matter to you and members of your board. Accordingly, after having been authorized to do so by Mr. Willard Robertson, chairman of the Board of Commissioners of the Authority, I am suggesting that the meeting be held Wednesday, July 6 or Thursday, July 7 at 3:00 P.M. in the Board room of the Authority's central office, 524 Camp Street. We will expect to be notified not later than Tuesday, July 5, of the date you have selected. (We are sending copies of this letter to members of your Board whose names we have, and request that you notify any who may have been omitted.)

In order to conserve time at the proposed meeting, I'll cover some of the high points in advance.

The script deals specifically with the Desire Project, but the opening lines—presumably for theatrical effect—contain pathos and drama, a crowd of youths and children gathered about a small Negro boy lying bleeding and neglected on the ground, near the cement curb his head had struck when he was hit by an automobile. It is made plain that the police and ambulance were telephoned for, but failed to respond for a lengthy period, inference being that the boy finally died because of this negligence. The script concluded a few pages later on with the removal of "the small, still form."

This incident is tied into what is described as the difficulty of getting in and out of the Desire Project, but it is not actually stated that this caused the police and ambulance to be so tardy.

After this opening nothing more is said about the accident victim until the script's conclusion, but it concentrates instead on a grossly exaggerated description of the project and its surroundings. The project is identified as a concentration camp, ". . . dreamed up by a city planner at Auschwitz." The Florida Avenue Canal is described as a large, muddy ditch half-filled with foul, garbage-infested water, "traversed by a lone, ancient, wooden bridge at Louisa Street." Reference is made to the project being surrounded by railroad tracks, a swamp, a smaller and muddier ditch than the Florida Avenue Canal, and Louisa Street, "full of holes." It is stated further, that, "All the streets in the concentration camp are an abomination," and "The area is covered with broken glass." Stress is laid upon lack of recreation facilities, including the statement that, "Last summer, several children from the project drowned in the bounding ditches attempting to swim after heavy rains." This portion of the script ends with the statement that at night there are few if any street lights.

The script contains some random charges, for example that youths dropped out of school to take emergency hurricane Betsy cleanup jobs; that, "The people of Desire are noticeably *black,* in a city where light-skinned Negroes have always been favored"; that, "Desire is the center in New Orleans of every social ill: crime, narcotics, unemployment, police brutality, despair, etc."

There are other statements in similar vein, all calculated to engender racial disharmony, notably, "There is no effective protest against the horror of these conditions. Minimal vote, minimal civic activity, no civil rights organization. No one speaks for the Ghetto of Desire. The situation parallels, almost as if planned, precisely that of Watts in Los Angeles before last summer's riots," and the final grim pronouncement (just before recounting the removal of the dead boy's body): "Some day, possibly very soon, the city of New Orleans will hear an explosion, and no one, not the political 'leaders', the police, the 'good' Negroes who have gone along with the game all this time in exchange for personal favors—no one will understand why. A particularly provoking arrest, a train which blocks exit or entrance too long, another death in the ditch—who can tell what will trigger the fuse."

As may readily be surmised, we are shocked at the prospect of so grossly unfair an image of the city of New Orleans, and specifically the Desire Project, being presented to the people of the United States. We cannot understand the motivation, nor can we comprehend what good may be anticipated. If there were evidence of willful neglect, of chronic mistreatment, of callousness in any other form on the part of the Authority leading to the conclusion that the thousands of residents of the Desire Project are, in effect, "abandoned" in spite of all reasonable efforts to arouse the Authority to a full sense of responsibility, then and only then could we look without too much suspicion and distrust upon what we must consider an infamous indictment.

On the contrary, as the enclosure [an official city document] will reveal, we have always exerted all possible efforts to make life rewarding and agreeable for the Desire residents, over and above standard habitations and rentals comfortably within their means. This, of course, is our policy in all projects. We possibly have tried to do somewhat more for the Desire Project than the others, recognizing the natural disadvantages of the project's location, and also its immense size. Even in the matter of police protection, in order to obtain adequate coverage we pay the salaries of police officers regularly assigned there.

As I pointed out to Mrs. Dreyfus, the principal victims of the smear, if it materializes, will be the people who live in the Desire Project, the great majority of whom are decent, productive, hardworking and in every respect worthwhile citizens. The average rent they pay is a bit higher than the overall program average, they send their children to schools and in hundreds of cases to colleges and universities, and generally represent a solid and respected segment of our community. If they have been more victimized than residents of other areas, or if—which is more likely—such occurrences have been more highly publicized (in certain instances by those interested in self-aggrandizement) they are more deserving then of consideration, and unwarranted stigmatization should not be added to their already heavy burden.

Our purpose in meeting with you and the other members of your Board is to present an earnest, and we believe highly justified request that the proposed presentation of the "Ghetto of Desire" by CBS be canceled. We prefer to achieve our objective in this manner, on the basis of amity and reason. Frankly, we not only will be disappointed and disenchanted if our request is refused, but will be constrained to resort promptly and determinedly to other measures to avoid the contemplated blight on this city's reputation and dignity.

Very truly yours,
Allen Dowling
Tenant Relations Advisor
Housing Authority of New Orleans

CC to following:

Mrs. Leonard Dreyfus
Dr. Richard Schechner
Mrs. Margaret Hellbach
Mr. Isaac Garrison
Miss Oretha Castle
Mrs. Timothy Slater
Rev. Milton Upton

Willard E. Robertson, Chairman
Ellie H. Schill, Vice-Chairman
Everett G. Collins, Commissioner
Harry J. Batt, Commissioner
A. P. Tureaud, Commissioner

J. Gilbert Scheib, Executive Director
George L. Bott, Deputy Executive Officer

July 6, 1966

Mr. Allen Dowling
Tenant Relations Advisor
Housing Authority of New Orleans

Dear Mr. Dowling:

I have received your letter of July 1, 1966.

It seems as if you are requesting a meeting with the Board of Directors of the Free Southern Theater. If you would care to put your request in the proper form, I shall be happy to take it up with members of our Board.

Because your letter indicated that you might not be familiar with the usual procedures in these matters, let me outline them for you:

1. In requesting a meeting with the governing body of a group, you should permit that group to suggest the time and place of the meeting;
2. You should make clear who is requesting the meeting. Exactly what "representatives" of the Housing Authority do you propose attend such a meeting?

It is most unusual for you to send letters to some members of our Board of Directors rather than contacting me directly. In the future, I suggest you write to me or our Board's secretary, Mrs. Margaret Hellbach.

Very truly yours,
Thomas C. Dent
Chairman

cc: Mr. Willard E. Robertson

July 7, 1966

Mr. Thomas C. Dent
Chairman
Board of Directors
Free Southern Theater, Inc.
Box 2374
New Orleans, Louisiana

Dear Mr. Dent:

This acknowledges your letter of July 6, 1966, in response to my letter of July 1.

In order to conform to the requirements you enumerated, I am stating herewith that I have been authorized by Mr. Willard

E. Robertson, chairman of the Board of Commissioners of the Authority, to request a meeting of the Authority's Board, and probably certain other Authority officials (Executive Director, Deputy Executive Officer, Attorney, and Tenant Relations Advisor) with you and members of your Board, and any other officials of your group you may desire to have present.

We request that the meeting be held within the next several days, and offer the Board room of the Authority's central office, 524 Camp Street, as the place for the meeting; or, if dictated by the number of persons in attendance, the Assembly Room, at the same address. As to the hour, an afternoon meeting would be our preference, but this is not absolutely necessary.

In view of the subject to be discussed, involving a time element, it is our feeling that the meeting should be called not later than Wednesday, July 13, 1966. We trust that you will share our point of view in respect to the urgent need for the meeting, and will expect to hear from you in the immediate future.

Yours very truly,
Allen Dowling,
Tenant Relations Advisor
Housing Authority of
New Orleans

cc:
Mr. Willard E. Robertson

July 13, 1966

Dear Mr. Dowling:

Thank you for your letter of July 7.

I have polled my Board of Directors and we do not feel that a meeting with representatives of the New Orleans Housing Authority would be productive.

Sincerely,
Thomas C. Dent
Chairman

TD *The Housing Authority was not amused. They sent representatives to New York to talk with the National Council of Churches in an effort to cancel the show, scheduled to be shown in August. The National Council stood behind the show, but it was blacked out in New Orleans.*

August 7, 1966

To The Members of the Free Southern Theatre,

This morning I was thoroughly shaken and moved by your performance on "Look Up and Live." You said a lot of things that are not heard often enough. Rather than abstractions and generalizations you offered personal feelings. The words of the "black woman soliloquy" where she expressed her disgust at being merely a "dish-washer, baby-breeder, etc." moved me to want to take an active part in making (the desire for) equality a real thing in this country. Thank you for your powerful and well performed program.

I would appreciate any literature on The Free Southern Theater you can send me.

Sincerely,
Ellen Rothberg
[South Norwalk, Connecticut]

September 13, 1966

Dear Sirs:

I recently saw your broadcast on CBS's "Look Up and Live." I was completely absorbed by the program; by the Negro mood and spirit. Being white, I have not had as much opportunity to know the Negro soul, through literature and song, as I would like. Your program strengthened my desire to know more. The text said things that have never been said, and should be considered; and things that have been said before, presented in a new and fresh way.

The Civil Rights cause was evident, however it was treated, not from the Black Power, marching attitude, but from the attitude of hearts of the people concerned.

If there is a written text to the Afro-American Poetry and Song program that you presented, I should like very much to own a copy for my own personal reading. Is this possible?

Thank you for your time and trouble, for your program, and for such a wonderful feeling.

Sincerely,
Karen Smith
[Dallas, Texas]

TD *Despite our conflicts it was a productive summer. We played in Mississippi, Alabama, Georgia, and New Orleans, capturing for many the spirit of black pride and consciousness that the Movement was also undergoing at that time.*

Many of the discussions after performances were fantastic, unforgettable. The Desire Project controversy usually, in New Orleans, led to a searching discussion of community organization and racial consciousness in that city, where black people have never thought of themselves as black. The show usually lasted a short 40 minutes, but the discussion went on for hours. Gil Moses' Roots *evoked good comments on the role of black men and black women. It was performed brilliantly by Roscoe and Denise. Plomer's short puppet play,* I Speak of Africa, *brought hoots of delight from black kids who saw themselves portrayed as heroes for the first time, and whites as crude villains. Brecht's* Does Man Help Man? *almost caused a fight in Atlanta at Morehouse's Sale Hall.*

July 24, 1966

Dear John and Mary,

In two weeks I shall be leaving the FST. Before you start

laughing, (after all my *Godot* type attempts to leave) try to understand that I must get away to think things over and that my decision is final for now. What I hope will happen is that next season I can return—perhaps with you.

It is too painful right now.

Movement people don't seem to have anything to say to me anymore. Before, when I first came down, the Movement had created certain definitions, they were the good guys (Movement) and the bad guys (crackers) (liberals) (whites who didn't do anything) (blacks who sold out). Now it seems that definitions are changing. Suddenly I am from the enemy—only to be looked at with mistrust—to be excluded. No one seems interested in the fact that I'm ready to give up my life too.

I'm not bitter, my friends, just hurt—but I'll get over it.

Murray

August, 1966

To the members of the Free Southern Theater:

The reflection I get from the FST up here is one of having "grown up." People no longer take a patronizing attitude towards it; but rather they think it is fantastic. And it is. More than they realize.

I have admiration for all of you who stuck it out—thru-out all the hassles—'cause I know how frustrating it is to take the time; to live thru, idea becoming reality.

You, this season, really have shot thru the arguments of all bullshit artists who are concerned, yet "steady making it." You have shot thru a whole history of the western concept of theater. In a sense, this season, you have done the most simple, yet impossible thing: provided an opening for young black artists; called into existence a theater which ignored commercialism; attempted to build an audience for expression where there was none . . . and you know all the other clouds and fog you have cut thru . . . precisely.

Personally, when I think of returning, the effort involved in the FST appears so great. IT IS SUCH AN EFFORT.

A theater so open that the internal and constant struggle between politics and art, between nationalism and internationalism, manifested itself externally—no other theater in this country can boast such scars, and pain.

I'm very proud that my play was part of your program. I was afraid you weren't going to do it. (And hey, can someone send me a few programs from the different cities?)

The problem is obviously staying together. After this year's experience, the art you could finally produce is fantastic.

I am all of a sudden overcome with the meaning of the theater, and the work of the people in it . . . and all I can finally say is: you deserve as much respect as any group or anybody I have ever known, heard of, or read about in my life; as much respect as a flower, as the sea, as change, as motion itself . . .

Gilbert

Part Five

DEPARTURES

TOM DENT'S JOURNAL

TD *Murray Levy came back the day after he left. If Murray had doubts about his role, Denise and Roscoe were suffering from battle fatigue, from laboring in a project which Denise later called "a rough, huge, bumbling thing that didn't allow one to really relax, to really go through things slowly, and work at things and prepare—like an artist is supposed to work." Denise and Roscoe left for good.*

The departure of these key people forced the Board of Directors, which now included several new people from New Orleans, to play a stronger role in determining the future of the theater. It was a role the Board was not prepared to play, but with the old leaders gone, there was no one else.

If 1966 was a solid step forward, 1967 represented a running in place. It was extremely difficult to find new people to carry on (with Murray and Bob Costley, who returned a little later) the work of the company. Administrative problems plagued us; most of the work had to be done by new recruits. Finally, in April 1967, we began our fifth season.

1967

Happy Ending
A one-act play
by Douglas Turner Ward

Uncle Tom's Second Line Funeral
An evening of poetry
compiled by the Company

The Lesson
by Eugene Ionesco

Company

Thomas Dent—actor, producer, director *(Uncle Tom's)*
Gary Boling—actor

Robert Costley—actor, director *(Ending)*
Jac'lyn Earley—actress
Murray Levy—actor, director *(Lesson)*
*Walter Lott—director
Cynthia McPherson—actress
*Walter Washington—guitarist
Carmel Collins—technical director
*George Hayes—technical director
Raymond DuVernay—technical assistant
David Henderson—poet in residence
Richard Aronson—general manager
John O'Neal
Richard Schechner

Apprentices:

Harold Campbell
Eric DuVernay
Joseph Alfred, Jr.
Sheilah Bland
Janet Givens

Community Workshop Program

*Carmel Collins—director
Eluard Burt—director
Raymond DuVernay—assistant director

* Involved for only portion of the time.

Gary Bolling—acting
Sylvia Hampton—acting
Lois Tillman—dance
Warren Parker—technical theater
Thomas Dent—writing
David Henderson—writing

Tour Schedule

April 30	—Sunflower, Miss. (Special preview for special elections in Sunflower County)
May 25–27	—New Orleans, La.
May 31–June 3	—New Orleans, La.
June 13–16	—LeMoyne College, Memphis, Tenn.
June 27–29	—Prairie View College, Prairie View, Texas
July 1–2	—Houston, Texas
July 5–6	—Southern University, Houston, Texas
July 8	—Xavier University, New Orleans, La.
July 11–14	—Tuskegee Institute, Tuskegee, Ala.
July 15	—Cordell, Ga.
July 16	—Albany, Ga.
July 18	—New Orleans, La.
July 21–22	—New Orleans, La.
July 28–29	—New Orleans, La.
August 4–5	—New Orleans, La.
August 11–12	—New Orleans, La.
August 26	—New Orleans, La.

Journal from 1967 Southern Tour

Tom Dent

April 30—Sunflower, Miss.

We were en route from New Orleans to Sunflower County, Mississippi. Early on a warm hopeful Sunday morning. Tomorrow in Sunflower there would be special elections. For the first time, in two towns, Moorhead and Sunflower City, the MFDP (Mississippi Freedom Democratic Party) was running black candidates with a chance to win.

We anticipated a six-hour drive. For most of the 1967 company (Walter Lott of New York City; Cynthia McPherson of San Francisco, Calif; Jac'lyn Earley of Cleveland, Ohio; Gary Bolling of New York City) this was a virgin visit to Mississippi. The veterans (Robert Costley of San Francisco and Buffalo, N. Y., and Murray Levy of New York City) had an air of renewed urgency.

We drove directly north through Jackson, through Yazoo City which is a gate to the Delta region, then 50 miles or so farther north to the small town of Moorhead, in the heart of the Delta. Green forest—forbidden—lonely—beautiful and desolate at the same time.

When we arrived there were people milling about: Black community people in their Sunday best humming with activity; Delta Ministry and LCDC (Lawyers Constitutional Defense Committee) workers; veteran Movement reporters like Bob Analavage and Bob Fletcher; the curious, especially teenagers, and us—excited and slightly frightened. A meeting of the county's black candidates and workers was in progress.

Our canvas sign went up. We unloaded our equipment. A teenager who had been gawking at us as if we were the circus laughed when I asked him, "Where's the nearest men's room?" Mrs. Lela Mae Brooks, who was running for alderman of Sunflower City, informed us we would stay overnight with her.

Sunflower County is famous because it is the home of Mrs. Fannie Lou Hamer. Sunflower County is also the home of the powerful racist, Senator James Eastland, who is the principal land owner. Widespread unemployment, as high as 75 per cent. The county 60 per cent black. Average income per year: $650. Government food distribution, but people can't afford the stamps. One notices something about these communities: the Delta is minus young black adults. The hearty who can work leave for more promising land.

In the afternoon, three miles from Moorhead in Sunflower City, we relaxed with Mrs. Brooks. Her home was modest but overflowing with excitement and food for everyone. The FDP had done a thorough job here. In both Moorhead and Sunflower City blacks had slight registered majorities. Mrs. Brooks told us she was fired from her job because of her activities. Mrs. Annie Mae King (also a candidate for alderman) had her home burned down. Twice in Indianola, the largest town in the county, SNCC Freedom Schools were burned to the ground. Mrs. Hamer's house in Ruleville, a few miles north of here, was shot up.

We went with Mrs. Brooks to meet Otis Brown, 21 years old and running for mayor of Sunflower City, arrested sixteen times. He lived in the community-built center a few houses down and did not expect us; we caught him reading his Bible. He rose—tall, thin, hooknosed, his manner impassive and irreverent. Somehow there had been a mixup in housing, Mrs. Brooks explained. Otis made an obscene comment about the inefficiency of the housing committee. Mrs. Brooks kept her cool—everything would be worked out. Otis had a seriousness of manner that one associates with rural, puritan upbringing. I liked him, but he seemed more interested in respect—and how to earn it.

Clear night, full of anticipation—an anticipation peculiar only to communities with raised fists. Later I went a block or two past the Community Center and was out of town. Miles of sparse, desolate, flat landscape. A cotton patch here, a cotton patch there. Hardly a wind. All this land, for that is so much what it is all about in the South, land and the threat of its slipping away from the white master's hands. People are starving right out there bold in the dust, the very old and the very young. They will take their land back. It isn't a question of "social justice" or "equal rights." Just power, the need for it cauterized by starvation, burned homes, and burned bodies.

That night we played in the Moorhead church, the church bursting with people, as many outside trying to see through the windows as inside. It seemed as if every black person in Moorhead and Sunflower was there—and several people drove up from Jackson. Walter, Cynthia, Murray, Jackie, and Gary improvised a poetry show about commitment—commitment, really, to being there. It was rushed and not well worked out, but our company was caught up in the Sunflower thing. (Mrs. Brooks liked to say, "We're gonna do something for our little Sunflower . . . we're gonna make it smile.") *They* were the show. Bob conducted a discussion afterwards. Elderly people talking "gonna be free," "A-men." A question arose about one of the poems which was unreligious in nature. Someone asked if the church was the place to present a poem like this. A woman answered, "Honey, life is what we make out of it."

We went to Sunflower's lone black café, a small place with no liquor and a poolroom in the rear where teenagers hang out. Shooting pool with Steve Scott, 19 years old, who wanted to join the company after the elections. He worked for Otis, had been arrested 14 times in demonstrations. Steve said, "No future for me here in Sunflower—have to get out."

"Have you finished high school?"

"Finished in Indianola (nine miles away), but I can't learn anything here. Have to get away where I can learn something. Never been anywhere but to Chicago once . . ."

That night some of us slept at the home of an old woman, a friend of Mrs. Brooks. She was lovely in her seventy-years—as defiant and determined as Otis Brown. It began to rain. Right then, Sunflower was the center of our universe.

One day in Sunflower placed the draining personality problems and administrative difficulties in New Orleans—everything—in perspective.

Flooding outside.

Here we are related to something more important than us, more important than theater. We play a role in the ascension of the black man in this world—it is an important one, but it is one spoke on the wheel.

Idea spoke.

Woman in audience, IN WHITE AMERICA, Holmes County, Miss., Summer, 1964

MATT HERRON

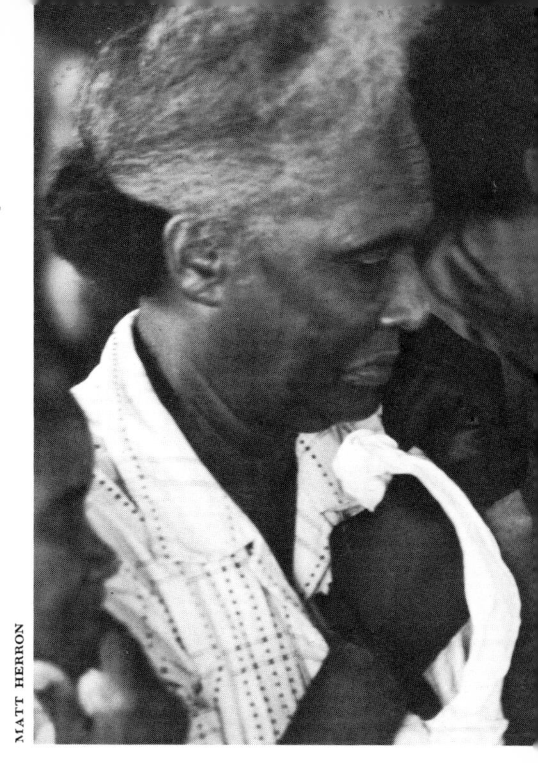

Man in audience, IN WHITE AMERICA, Holmes County, Miss., Summer, 1964

MATT HERRON

DENNIS J. CIPNIC

Woman in audience, GHETTO OF DESIRE TV poetry show, New Orleans, June, 1966

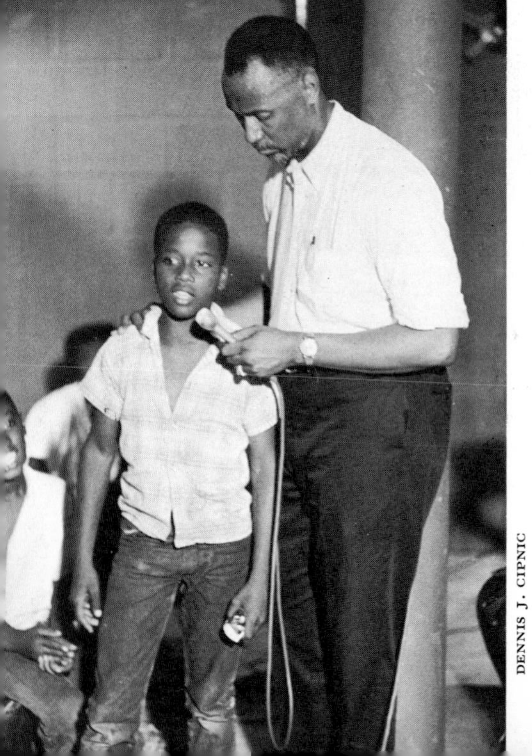

DENNIS J. CIPNIC

Robert Costley holding mike for comments of Tony Petite, GHETTO OF DESIRE TV poetry show, New Orleans, June,1966

DENNIS J. CIPNIC

Audience, GHETTO OF DESIRE TV poetry show, New Orleans, June, 1966

DENNIS J. CIPNIC

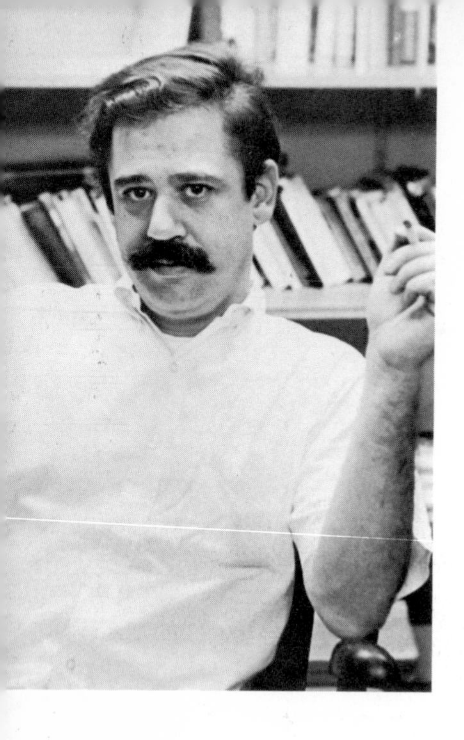

Richard Schechner

Audience, GHETTO OF DESIRE TV poetry show, New Orleans, June, 1966

DENNIS J. CIPNIC

Audience shots, Holmes County, Miss., Summer, 1964

MATT HERRON

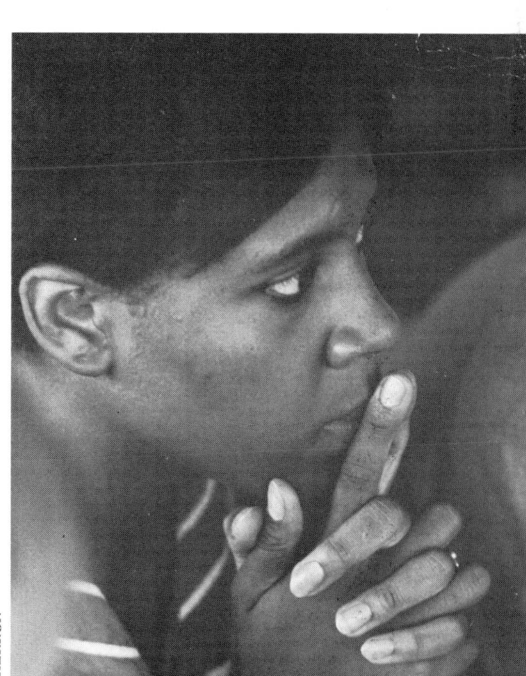

MATT HERRON

MATT HERRON

Free Southern Theater building, Desire area, New Orleans, Summer, 1968. Tom Dent in background.

Karate Club, Free Southern Theater building, Summer community

MATT HERRON

(left to right) Robert Cordier, Mathilde Sheppard and Emalyn Hawkins, at rehearsal, New Orleans, Summer, 1965

workshop program, 1968

MATT HERRON

DENNIS J. CIPNI

Audience, GHETTO OF DESIRE TV poetry show, New Orleans, June, 1966

Neighbor of the Free Southern Theater, Desire area, New Orleans, Summer, 1968

MATT HERRON

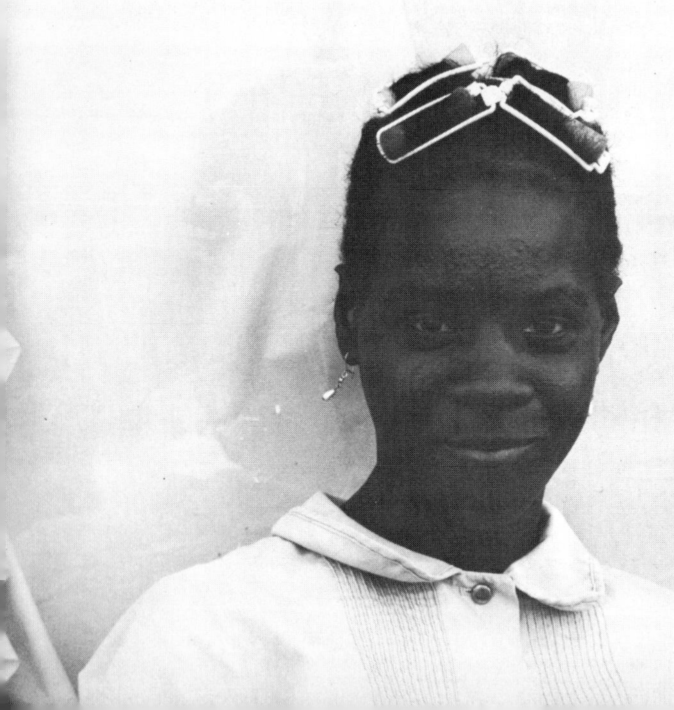

Desire Housing Project, New Orleans, Summer, 1968

MATT HERRON

Courtyard, Desire Housing Project, New Orleans, Summer, 1968

MATT HERRON

MATT HERRON

Desire Street and Florida Avenue, New Orleans, Summer, 1968

Neighbors of the Free Southern Theater, Desire area, New Orleans, Summer, 1968

MATT HERR

Neighbor of the Free Southern Theater, Desire area, New Orleans, Summer 1968

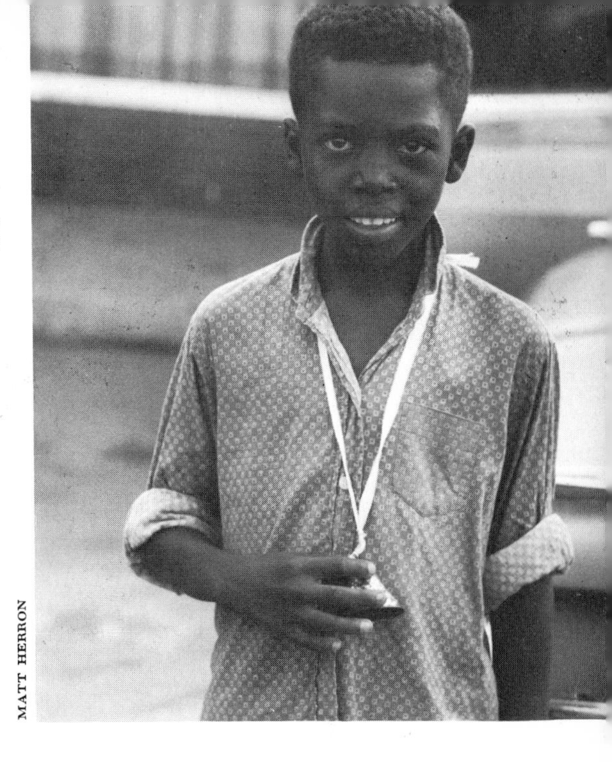

MATT HERRON

An observer at rehearsal, Texas Southern University, Houston, Texas, July, 1967

RICHARD PIPES

MATT HERR

Audience, Holmes County, Miss., Summer, 1964

The houses in Sunflower are built on stilts so they won't float away when it floods.

Sunflower is where we belong with its shacks, dirt roads, wooden churches, old women talking about being free and pool-shooting teenagers who want to learn something. The thunder here sounds like it's trying to tell white Mississippi something. The next morning we left early. Six weeks in New Orleans, then on the road again.

June 12—Memphis, Tenn.

This was the real tour: first to Memphis, then to Texas for the first time in our short history, finally to Alabama and Georgia. What a strange sadness the night before we left for Memphis. I missed Denise, Roscoe, Gil, John: to undertake a tour without them seemed inappropriate and full of foreboding. It had been a painful six weeks in New Orleans since Sunflower. (Incidentally, all the county MFDP candidates lost by small margins.) Of the three shows we hoped to have ready, only *Happy Ending* was halfway ready. We had been playing in New Orleans every week but the shows were uneven and unsteady. The company was suffering from nervous exhaustion. We faced an almost solid two months' tour with a new company under vastly differing conditions. Walter Lott had returned to New York, taking away an experienced director.

We left that morning at 6:00 A.M. I was the last person out. This had to be a new company for Bob, our company manager, to have gotten everyone up so early; the old gang would still be sleeping. Later I discovered no one really slept but me.

We drove through Hattiesburg to Jackson, then north to Memphis via U.S. 51, the highway of the Meredith march. Driving through Mississippi was never boring, not because of the spellbinding scenery, but because we had to be on the alert for the police. The countryside interesting enough—black faces and bodies that drag through motions, insulated from the outside world, numerous creeks and rivers as we flash by, names that amuse us (Big Black River, Little Black River, Jump Off Creek), historic towns that were famous battlegrounds in wars of the 1860s and 1960s. The Pearl River winding its way around our route northward like a snake as we keep a wary eye out for the State Patrol and dig Freedom Talk No. 24 on the radio . . . weirdos, beatniks, and well-dressed traitors are seducing our youth by teaching them that disloyalty and unnatural behavior are all right in our very midst without our knowing it. Beware! Back to gospel time.

American Oil / Mobil Oil / Gulf Oil / black faces popping out of roadside shacks to stare at the highway. Texaco Oil / Space Development Center. Vote for John Bell Williams. All know where he stands.

Finally the highway broadens, then Memphis just ahead. It looks like a small Atlanta. No anticipation or excitement. Just fatigue. This is a *working* tour. Tomorrow we will christen a brand-new theater on the LeMoyne College Campus. Terribly hot, hotter than New Orleans. We are hungry. Where does one eat in Memphis? Our clothes sticky / wet. It had been an eleven-hour drive—no car trouble—a hell of a lot to do and no time.

June 13—Memphis, Tenn.

Last night's attempt at a poetry rehearsal was a total failure—everyone was in an ugly and tense mood. I decided to try to reconstruct the show, a frightening idea because of my inexperience. Hopefully, we can add new material later. After breakfast we met the LeMoyne summer theater director, who was cordial, white, and just out of Tulane. (Many of the summer personnel here seem to be white, a commentary on "integration" in the Negro colleges which have almost no white students. Negro colleges seem to think they became more important in proportion to the percentage of white teachers. Someone should write a play about that.)

Not long after we began unpacking Jackie was in tears, the result of a terrible argument with Bob. It is impossible to convey how hot it was—clothes were an absolute burden. Jackie is young, fiercely independent—Bob had accused her of insubordination and she was ready that minute to leave the theater. Maybe in another theater she would have *had* to leave, but we were opening *Happy Ending,* in which Jackie had a key part, that afternoon—we had two rehearsals scheduled after the performance.

Bob, in his early forties, spending his third year with this circus, was in a wave of depression. He believed we had blown the entire season already: organizing the company in three different cities, rushing without sufficient funds—no time to think about how things would work out. The company wasn't functioning as a unit. I tended to agree with Bob; it was hopeless, but maybe being on the road would force us to work together.

Nevertheless, here we are, having to get through the LeMoyne shows. We don't have another actress who can immediately replace Jackie and she knows it, so she has agreed to stay at least through Memphis. We open to a moderately full house of students and faculty. I give my usual introductory talk about FST, its work, etc. I always try to set an informal, non-theatrical atmosphere. It doesn't seem to work here. Then Costley says a word about the play and the actors.

Ellie and Vi are crying at the opening of *Happy Ending.* Cynthia and Jackie are, as James Cleveland says, "really real"; in fact it is so damn morbid I begin to wonder if they can come out of it. Suddenly, especially Gary as the youth, we have the audience. But these people are restrained; nothing like the raucous outbursts the play received in New Orleans. After all, this is a college audience and if you laugh too hard people might think you're not cultured.

In company meeting backstage, I tell everyone it was a good try, but I will recommend to the Board of Directors that we cancel the tour after Memphis. We will in all probability remain in New Orleans and just do community workshops, meaning only a few people will remain. Reaction: silence and resignation.

Later we had a marvelously spirited rehearsal, as if everyone was overcome by a Mardi Gras of release from tension. Second thoughts about canceling the season. After all, we are committed to dates; maybe we can play out our troubles. We are all exhausted and need rest to think things over . . . but there is no time.

An intelligent and volatile young man from New Orleans, Raymond DuVernay, has joined us as technician and stage manager. An intractable chauvinist about his favorite New Orleans foods, especially seafood. After rehearsal we cruise Memphis searching for "Oriental gumbo" which, someone has told Raymond, exists at a Chinese seafood house. We drew strange stares asking pedestrians for directions to this place, but Raymond is determined—besides, whatever it is it sounds good. Finally we give up and settle on a barbecue place which looks far too clean. The barbecue, naturally, is horrible; they don't even have ribs; it is owned by *Pat Boone* and you can smell it a block away. Ray: "Man, Memphis is so jive." Gary: "Even *Harlem* got barbecue." We get directions from a cat and finally find it. On Hernando Street, near Beale. It has the real taste, but—Ray's verdict: strictly third rate.

June 14—Memphis, Tenn.

This afternoon we did our first rehearsal performance of Ionesco's *The Lesson.* Murray was terribly apprehensive but did an effective Professor. It was his birthday . . . I have never seen him more depressed after a performance. As Pupil, Jackie exhibited fine control and seemed to have recovered from the previous day's histrionics. Murray must be going through hell. A veteran of *Waiting for Godot,* he has been with the troupe longer than any of the present group. Murray put down the N.Y. stage in the name of black people and FST. He is the only white actor remaining in a company which was once more than half white. We have debated and argued for almost two years now the role of white people in what we have come to consider a Black Southern Theater—we have spilled our blood all over the black-white argument until—well now, here in June 1967, we are too drained to talk about it. I am the first one to admit no one has been more dedicated to FST than Murray, but Murray knows I have serious reservations about the propriety and usefulness of his being here. The reservations are hardening into convictions. Not the same situation as 1964 when the Movement was easy to define and everyone could sign Movement letters "Up the Rebs." We are now in an essential stage when black people must run their own movements and organizations. In too many ways we are still going through the *motions* of 1964.

A question from the Dean (who is black) during the discussion of *The Lesson:* "Are you not doing violence to the spirit of Ionesco's play by minor alterations in the script to give it a racial application?"

Answer: "No, at least not in theory, though in this case the particular changes we made may not work as well as we would like." We try to make productions apply particularly to black audiences. We decided to try *The Lesson* because we thought it had special relevance for the colleges we would tour. It was one of our liveliest discussions. It continued into the cafeteria where several students commented that the Dean resembled Ionesco's Professor.

Today Jackie is guardedly optimistic about staying with the company. Costley still doubtful about our chances of success; Murray, depressed and non-communicative; Dick Aronson, our temporary general manager, cheerful by telephone from New Orleans.

Gary Bolling has found a chick. She wears a smart natural—so striking in conventional Memphis. A singer in a local jazz club. Gary has—well, sex appeal. He is going to be a big star some day; at 20 he has already considerable technique under his belt. Dig the way he makes the audience howl in *Happy Ending* and pulls off the big transition in the script. He learned his stuff in Harlem—at HarYou and the New Lafayette Theater. This is his first time South. He really has this chick, she's making noises like she wants to become an actress, join the company, etc. I will check Gary's impressions of Miss Natural a little later in the summer after he has had time to evaluate her more carefully.

Memphis heat unbelievable; little relief during the day. The ramshackle house where we stay might once have been the hospital of a Negro physician. With no fans or air conditioning, it is at least 90° at night. I don't get much sleep. One night I gave up trying and drove all over Memphis. About 3:00 A.M. I got lost and couldn't find my way back to the college. I must have been in Arkansas. I hate to ask directions. It was daybreak before I hit familiar streets.

Whether or not we should try to work it through this summer's schedule is constantly on my mind. If it's at all possible I want to, and I know I must make the decision, and I don't want to. Why is every blessed week with FST an emergency, a crisis which taxes everyone to exhaustion and leaves us too weary even to sleep? We must all be some unspecified type of masochist.

LeMoyne is a very small college with no dormitory students. Many black students who once might have attended LeMoyne now matriculate at integrated Memphis State, which is huge. Most people in the summer program are in Upward Bound, an 8-week pre-college preparatory program, with a few conspicuous white youths. You can see startlingly new buildings interspersed with old red brick and wooden ones. Surrounding the campus are the shacks and government projects of the black ghetto. You can look out at the shacks of Memphis through plate-glass windows in the new student activities building. At night the students are all gone and there is no activity. The house where we stay is a summer home for a few athletes. Quiet, tall, subdued boys who watch TV constantly.

The town shows signs of black prosperity and sophistication, many excellent night spots. Music bluesy and good. Beale Street like Rampart in New Orleans—or like Rampart was before it was urban renewed. Pawn shops, cheap clothing stores, notions shops, dingy drug stores: where black people own nothing but bring all their pennies each week. W. C. Handy Park at the end of Beale is a mini-square and ill-kept. It, apparently, is what the white powers of Memphis think of Handy.

June 15—Memphis, Tenn.

Our poetry show went well, though it is too short. We built the script around Robert Hayden's "Runagate, Runagate." We still lack the piece to bring the show home *now*, and don't know where we will find it.

June 16—Memphis, Tenn.

Today was the eleventh time we did *Happy Ending* and the best, a beautiful enthusiastic job by Cynthia, Jackie, Gary, and Bob before an audience hanging on every word. They got the nuances and dug every bit of it, especially the generation battle the script touches on. Some people from the Front Street Theater in Memphis came. They had been involved in the Chicago production of *Happy Ending* and *Day of Absence*. They said they liked ours—it was the best production of *Happy Ending* they had seen. If so it was because of the audience, playing before an audience of black youths who understand and have lived through what Ward is talking about.

I am now convinced we should go through with our Texas dates and, despite all our problems, try to complete the season. We leave early tomorrow morning for New Orleans. We will have a few days off before we resume rehearsals for Texas.

A lovely last meal in the LeMoyne cafeteria, prepared by the cafeteria manager, a woman who was most gracious and seemed to understand what we were all about. We left Memphis exhausted, slightly older, and with good feeling.

Monday, June 26—en route to Prairie View, Texas

We left late Monday morning, this time with an additional technician, an old friend Carmel Collins, who has returned from New York where he lived for several years. We were also breaking in a new two-day-old Chevy mini-bus, which we call "the Greyhound."

June 21—along River Highway La. 18,
north of New Orleans, La.

Uneventful trip back from Memphis. Cynthia's gone, we assume to Chicago. We will all return to New Orleans in four or five days to leave for Texas. Driving through Kenner to Harrahan, then across the river on a small, slow ferry, in the car, seeming lightyears away from urbanity, the river muddy and filled with debris, logs, floating pieces of wood. The low chug-a-lug of the ferry's motor, docking on the Luling side by rope, the jolt of the ferry as it hits the dock, then along side the Mississippi River northwestward on La. 18.

How unglamorous we are this year. Here we are in the middle of something, no one's excited about us being in the South anymore, the action in the urban centers, neglected during the early sixties, is now exploding. The South's not where it is now. America doesn't care about Luling or Sunflower or Jackson, America cares about explosions and fires, white America has her torch lighted to spot the dollar; we must burn and loot the dollar. Slow, winding drive up the river toward Donaldsonville, the water blocked from view by the levee. Whites, country whites, flood into the French Quarter on weekend nights, buy dollar take-out drinks, toss their pennies here and there, look for someone to screw—last week a black kid, one of those few left in the Quarter, shot in the head by rednecks in a passing car which roared off into the swamps—his angry friends arrested by the cops for their anger. Past Hahnville, Kilona, Edgard; you must watch the sharp curves. These are the oldest settlements in Louisiana, settlements founded by the French, Germans, Arcadians, who came to drive out the Indians and bring *civilization,* Louisiana historical markers tell us. Always it is the shacks of black people closest to the river, closest to the longest, muddiest, baddest river: one sign by the road near Hahnville notes that a huge mansion existed here in the 18th Century. Now the very sight of this landmark of Western civilization swept away and swallowed by the Mississippi which never stands still. Black people still refer to the places they live in these settlements as "plantations." To the left of the highway nothing but swamp and trees, settlements penetrate the foliage only a half-mile or so. The river smells stagnant; where oil developments located the smell putrid. Edgard has a country store which is also the bus stop, the store has a porch for black people waiting, always, for the bus to New Orleans; waiting like in *Day of Absence.* Sometimes you see a huge white mansion with its surrounding shacks, left over from the old days. In Mississippi one rarely sees black service station attendants; those jobs don't exist for us. Louisiana is different: Gov. McKeithen proudly points to "progress in our beautiful state," leaders of the black community applaud.

The river controls everything, roads and shacks are shaped by it, commerce too. Soon we must get ourselves together for Texas.

Feel myself unwind slowly as the river road winds just as slowly northward. The river will be here a long time, has been here a long time, may as well relax and get with it.

On weekends the radio brings us Monitor, canned music, ideas and comment prepared for all of America, even rural Louisiana.

During the week we listen to WYLD, the soul station in New Orleans. Larry McKinley plays the records and we listen to him sell wigs, permanents, rings, TV (no money down, no credit required), houses (get away from that old crowded neighborhood). James Brown lays down the James Brown, clouds dance and waves from ships in the river wash up old logs into swamp. Someone said the only music that could possibly have come out of the Mississippi Delta is the blues. Monk is tenement music, the music of tightly constructed buildings and streets. The blues (with winding beat) is the music of river road and the shacks beside it, and the river washing away what it doesn't like.

We will perform three nights at Prairie View A & M College, about 50 miles from Houston, one of the oldest Negro land grant colleges in Texas. The following week we will play in Houston; first in the city, later at Texas Southern University.

On the way to Prairie View we detoured to the home of Rhonda Dreyfus, one of our directors, for a barbecue dinner. Arrived in Prairie View 10:00 P.M. I have not been here since the summer of 1952, when it was considered a small, "country" school. We were met, surprisingly, by a delegation of students and their advisor, Horace Bond, who showed us to dormitories where we would stay. Floyd Gaffney of Ohio University, who is completing a study of our theater and Karamu House in Cleveland, had come to see the Prairie View shows.

Prairie View has grown immensely. As at Texas Southern, money has been lavishly splashed about by the state to hold down the number of black students registered in white state universities. At least eight or ten new buildings in the last decade, a stark contrast to the older, time-worn structures which in pre-desegregation times served the school. Student body and faculty have increased proportionally.

As in Memphis, terrible, oppressive heat which must be felt to be believed. During the day in the open, flat plains of the campus it is at least a hundred. The campus has a happy, busy sound in contrast to LeMoyne. Gary, Carmel, Gaffney, Costley, Raymond, and myself stay in a modern men's dormitory with air-conditioning full blast all the time, which made it about 80° inside during the day. And at night, when the heat lightened up it felt like 32°.

We offered to do a discussion workshop with interested students in the afternoon before the shows. We talked about black writers, the Movement, the FST, anything they wanted to discuss. Tuesday afternoon Bond brought his "experiment in living" class, high school valedictorians from throughout the state enrolled in a special pre-college program at Prairie View. How meek and quiet they were, particularly on the racial struggle. One reflects on the changes a youth must go through to become a high school valedictorian. Only two of the twenty had read books by black authors. (One high school teacher in another class had said she thought LeRoi Jones' *Dutchman* "had something to do with race . . . with the racial situation.") Two-thirds of the group had performed in high school productions, but none had been in plays by a black writer. None had used a book by a Negro writer in class. Racial discussion and black history are suppressed. Do not discuss, do not question, you will succeed in high school.

At one afternoon session Cynthia and I entertained a young man who planned to enter Prairie View in September 1967 as a major in animal science. He explained that this is the science of slaughtering animals and mastering the other disciplines necessary for the preparation of meat for the market. His ambition, he said, was to become a meat inspector. He was a very dark young man about eighteen and from rural eastern Texas. His family owned land and livestock. Both Cynthia and I marveled at his pride in his capacity for slaughtering pigs; he explained in gory detail how it is done. As we talked with him further he told us his mother wanted him to be a meat inspector; secretly he would like to study law.

We saw a few white students who lived near Prairie View and were taking summer courses. For the most part they had little contact with the black students, even in the dormitories.

Happy Ending received a rousing ovation. The poetry show went fairly well to a smaller audience. *The Lesson* suffered from inadequate preparation and playing in the barn-like atmosphere of the gymnasium, and the students tolerated us until a dance began. A few students dug the theater and came every night. Most seemed not to care—their evenings were important to them for other purposes.

Once again, as we attempted rehearsals, discussion workshops, and shows under vastly varying circumstances we hardly had time to think. We cannot ever correct all our mistakes, and every situation presented new circumstances, making mistakes inevitable. Had we known better we would not have attempted *The Lesson,* in which language is so important, in the gymnasium where acoustics are terrible. We got burned. In gyms and outdoors, we learned we must use a mike, which we don't have. Mistakes hurt morale, but somehow we don't know *how* to avoid them.

Every situation this summer is approached on the most elementary level.

Prairie View is delightful. Hempstead, the closest town to Prairie View, is the watermelon capital of the world. As you approach Hempstead, the highway is littered with watermelon stands. Watermelons in Hempstead come in all sizes and varieties: striped, solid green, oblong, round, yeallow meat. According to Horace Bond, the watermelon growing in Hempstead has achieved the status of an aesthetic, and watermelon swiping among some of our Prairie View student friends was a favorite sport. I recommend yeallow meat.

The same with barbecue, an aesthetic in Texas. First prize for the tour so far: a Hempstead place owned by a black woman who knows how to smoke it and promote it. She has an ancient pit constructed from something that looks like an airplane fuselage. Sawdust floor, West Indian movie décor, and all varieties of barbecue, including barbecued beans. Customers come from thirty miles around. She had an old 1890 cash register that made you think she couldn't do no better. One day she had to change a ten and went out to the back yard, opened the trunk of her 1968 Cadillac, and flipped through a whole tool box of bills.

The big Prairie View hangout is a café-motel about a mile from the campus. Good Texas blues band—jammed every night. Black people everywhere we go groove to soul music. Every town cooks *Summertime* differently, each town with its own recipe. All part of the same stew. Tastes good everywhere we go.

July 1—Houston, Texas

We arrived in Houston early this afternoon. Now we are trying to settle housing problems, as all our prior arrangements seem to have fallen through. Finally we decided everyone will stay at a hotel except myself. I'm staying at the home of my cousin, Dr. Emory Covington. We are to play two shows under the auspices of the Houston Council of Human Relations Saturday and Sunday. On Wednesday and Thursday we move our tents to Texas Southern University.

Saturday night we played our first street performance in a ghetto area where Vista workers were operating a neighborhood carnival. We blocked off the street and made the driveway of their house our stage. People brought chairs from their homes; plenty of room for the audience in the street auditorium. We did the poetry show. We learned for this kind of show we *had* to have a mike, and when we added the wonderful young soul singer and guitarist, Walter Washington, he alone, with his amplified guitar, created an instant audience. Kids always make noise; the actors have to learn to keep their cool.

Of course what we need to move toward in our "open" shows is a format that can induce the same audience response and litany that our musicians get, a performer-audience dialogue basic to black art that stems from the preacher-congregation rhythms of the Negro church. Our poems, even if militant and well done, are still too formal, too much like recitation pieces to command instantaneous audience response. Music and singers can do this, but we need to arrive at a form loose enough to allow the performers to groove with whatever the audience feels, loose enough to be adaptable to different situations. Outdoors, we not only must present solid and exciting material, but must capture and hold the attention of the audience. Street shows are important because we can reach people we might never reach in an auditorium or a church. In any case our theater usually becomes a circus—the performers confronted with people, especially children, who wander in and out at will, under the best of conditions. And who feel free, as they should, to talk and react vigorously to what happens on stage. Productions that work best have clearly defined and evocative imagery, and I think it is in this direction that black theater must develop. After all, black people are accustomed, in church music, to extremely emotional art, extremely demonstrative responses. I would think that in the black theater of the future, music will play a strong role.

Though our first poetry show in Houston in the driveway was performed under good conditions and went rather well, when we played *Happy Ending* on the basketball court of Tuffly Park the next night we were overwhelmed with running kids who, midway through the play, resumed their basketball game. Once again working without mikes hurt us, and the actors were forced to shout their way through the script.

NOTE: In future tours we *must* have a tour manager who can size up performance conditions beforehand and try both to alert the company and adapt the site so we can make the best of each situation. Also someone to take care of the many administrative details of booking, housing, payment if we're getting paid, transportation, etc. All these details are a tremendous burden to artistic personnel, who have enough problems trying to get themselves up for performance. If we must ready a new show on the road, to do anything else becomes almost impossible.

Houston is large, unwieldy, booming with new Negro business. All the paraphernalia of the metropolis, including the maze of freeways. Yet you see many black ghettos which could explode like Texas Southern University did in the spring (1967). What massive paradoxes: Emancipation Park on Dowling Street with its humble facilities, the ease and ostentatiousness of expensive black middle-class homes, some complete with swimming pools, streets in neglected black areas with holes big as craters on the moon, the latest, plushiest, classiest colored clubs. In Texas money does the talking, for black people too. One could be a millionaire in Texas and still sound poor, and feel poor. All the growing trouble roots of Watts, Detroit, Newark, Harlem are in Houston: tremendous material growth for a few but not for the masses, no cultural awareness, no strong racial organization to protest social injustices. The influential black people are comfortable; the concerns of the lone Negro weekly, the *Houston Informer*, remain the same—crime, sex, mixtures of both, social news.

Houston, with its notable progress for black people . . . more jobs . . . more cars . . . more buildings . . . more youth in school . . . is typical of so much of the South we have seen this summer. But at the same time there is a pervasive ignorance about how these gains came about and how they are to be used. And so much of the old self-defeating psychology, the old fears of the omnipotent white man. Why is it, for example, that in the most affluent of Southern cities, the most violent explosion should occur at one of those growing, booming Southern state colleges? Yet no Negro with money or influence has come to the public defense of the TSU students who were arrested in April—and the black affluent class has not used its influence to keep the police in check when militant Negro protest is suppressed by force.

While I was in Houston I wanted to hold and tape a discussion on the TSU student "riot." I tried to get together some members of the faculty and a few other people who knew what had happened. Privately, many of these people said, "We know we didn't have a student riot. We had a police riot." And many were quick to come to the defense of the students, five of whom are now charged with murder under a Texas statute which states one can be charged even if he himself did not commit the crime but nevertheless "*caused*" it to come about. I had hoped to do the taping at the home of a close friend who is a professor. But I had difficulty setting up the date and when I pushed him about it, he explained that the university had already appointed an official committee to "investigate the riot" and he didn't want to "undercut" the committee. I was stunned but I shouldn't have been.

What concerns me is that I am sure this reluctance to talk forthrightly and publicly about crucial issues is not limited to my faculty member friend, but is extremely widespread. This oppressive silence and fear is present in the midst of the boom of business, buildings, jobs, "progress," etc. What kind of progress is this, that does not alleviate silence, fear, sustained self-hatred and insecurity?

We spent July 4 at the home of new-found friends, Willie Bright and his family. Bright attended our Saturday afternoon street show and had seen the theater on the August 1966 "Look Up and Live" TV program. Bright and Cynthia got into a long, hot discussion about black men-women relations, emasculation of Negro man by Negro woman, etc. Later that afternoon we drove to the beautiful beach of Galveston on the Gulf of Mexico, but it was gloomy and cloudy, crowded like Coney Island.

July 5—Houston, Texas

Tonight we opened at Texas Southern University. While we're here we will play exclusively for the Upward Bound program. We settled into an interesting discussion the first night after the performance over whether *Happy Ending* condoned stealing. One girl said she would never "lower" herself to thievery like Ellie and Vi did. When questioned, she said she had no domestics in her family. One boy said he was proud of the domestics in *his* family. This pride was intense with many articulate kids. The *Houston Chronicle* (George New) said "... in its fast-paced version of Ward's biting comedy Wednesday evening, the troupe was living up to its credo of not divorcing art from the essential concerns of black people: justice, full equality, re-education, self-analysis and strength." It was our only review by the white press during the entire summer tour. The following night we did *The Lesson*, followed by a part of the poetry show. Afterwards some students brought us a bucket of fried chicken and we were off to a party.

Tomorrow we leave Texas. None of the problems which threatened to wreck us in Memphis have been solved, or appear *near* solution. This despite my hope that we would work into a smoother unit under pressure, and despite my belief that even with imperfect shows and inadequate time to prepare for this kind of tour, there would be enough value in playing—enough in just being before an audience—*our* audience.

The pressures of the tour have not helped to diffuse our personality conflicts. Tonight, after the party, another violent, bitter argument almost burned down the Greyhound. The emotional energy that goes into this kind of thing just exhausts everyone, leaves us spent and frustrated. Without the money to afford decent travel and privacy we live too close to each other, vent our hostilities and disappointments against each other, again and again.

July 10—Tuskegee, Alabama

We are veterans of the Southern soil now. This particular soil is red clay, prosperous, and famous. Tuskegee is sedate, secure, and rather quiet. Our accommodations at Dorothy Hall Guest House are excellent. Julius Novick of *The Nation* has joined us for three days.

We did *The Lesson* first and got through it without too much difficulty in Tuskegee's Little Theater. Little or no publicity about our appearance . . . audience small. *Happy Ending* before a much larger audience generated a good discussion on how the roles of the Negro man and Negro woman have developed under the racial oppressions of American society. A good hot debate followed around whether Ellie or Vi are still dependent on the Harrisons at the conclusion of the play.

I imagine that the season is over, that I am free, that I can enjoy the physical beauty of this place. I imagine that we have a *play,* either I have written it or someone else, and it says what we must say; that there is no need for discussions or explanations, or even advertisements, that every black person in the South knows our role.

I am becoming acutely aware of a resentment and reluctance on my part and the company's to mount the discussion at all. The play is one kind of theatrical performance, the discussions another, which we must quickly shift into, feigning real interest in what the audience has to say about the play. We *are* interested in what the audience has to say; but we want to talk about anything but the play. The theatrical experience cannot be verbalized; we can't "do" it and then explain it. Why do it if you have to explain it? If we have them, if we have the audience, if they are floating along on the wings of the drama's quest, then we will know it, the senses tell. Somehow after we've really "done" it, on those rare occasions when simpatico occurs, it is profane to discuss it, to analyze it . . . it is much, much better to say to people, "Where in this town do you get good barbecue?" And if you have given them something they will tell you, and you will leave arm in arm with them and go out together and enjoy.

This is my dream of the theater. Of the Free Southern Theater. That it will fly on its own wings, that it will transcend its own ideological statements and speak on that level that only whisperers, lovers, and comics understand, that level of not just truth but celebration of life, of our lives if you please (the little ideological voice in the back of my head says), that it will not wash away the morning after that.

For us, I do not see this as purely an artistic question. It will come when we can forget about where the money will come from to operate tomorrow, the forms and details that should have been completed yesterday; it will come when we can dam, just for a little while, all the little worries and disputes that inundate us on this tour, so that the art can fly unfettered.

Last night, during the discussion of *Happy Ending* which swept up and finally overflowed beyond the play, we found ourselves saying that *Happy Ending* is really not *our* play. When I say "our" I mean this theater must have its own thing, its own illustration, depiction, if you will, not that it shuts the door for others to understand and not that others might not be the ones to create it. Ideology and political statement either through documentary or contemporary application are one thing; we, however, are in search of mythology. What is the mythology of our experience? We are in search of central rivers, the veins and arteries. The blood of the experience our people know, in all its joy and hurt, must flow on the stage. Then there will be no need of discussions. Finally, when DuVernay said, "We should stop defending *Happy Ending*, even if we play it, because it is all we have *now*," we understand that he was right. What happens on stage must define the emotions correctly; this is why Brecht's *Does Man Help Man?* worked in 1966. It exploded basic emotions in the minds of our audiences, though it wasn't written racially and it isn't contemporary. It touched something deep in the social order—not just *this* social order, but the larger, national social order—it hit race, then spiraled out similar conflicts like ever-expanding concentric circles. This is what we need, for we must not only *be* black, which means accepting our reality, as artists we must *use* it; it must become a device, a lever, a power which applies to reality in general. Or other realities. It must become a mythology. Tuskegee has defined the issues for us: we are still, like martinets, going through the motions of museum theater.

One further comment: black theater can be the way for us to achieve this mythology, a much quicker way than literature. The ingredients of theater are already strongly implanted in our culture: the music, the dance, the conflicts, the visual imagery, the evocative devices, are already there. We are not and have not been a reading people. This may be good, it may be not good; it is a fact. But theater can transcend this, it can develop, exploit what we have . . . now.

July 14—Tuskegee, Alabama

Yesterday David Henderson, the brilliant young narrative poet from New York, joined us. We have been using his "Keep on Pushing" (about the Harlem riot of 1964) in our poetry show. He will read as part of our repertory and work with our community writers' workshop when we return to New Orleans.

NOTE: The images and conflicts of modern white writers are rarely recognizable or important to black audiences. Take, for instance, sexuality. Many great contemporary plays deal with conflicts revolving around or symbolized by sexuality. To black audiences this is not a crucial matter. Problems of sexuality do exist among black people, but they haven't come to mean the same thing, haven't come near the obsessive extremes of European and white American culture.

Individual conflicts—conflicts arising out of individual basics in white American and European society are superseded in black art by conflicts arising out of the exigencies of group survival. The black man in America is never first a tall man, moody man, happy man, etc. He is always *first* (to whites) a "nigger." This is his first reality. He has to deal with it whether he wishes to or not. Even black people who think they are not dealing with it are.

This particular discussion came up last night after our poetry show (done, this time, with amplification) in the Tuskegee gymnasium. The discussion centered around the meaning and the values of black poetry. The occasion for intense debate (as we have so often observed) was the presence of several white Vista workers, one of whom remarked, "There's no such thing as black or white poetry; poetry is poetry." This always sets it off. A discussion ensued over how a black poet writing about spring might have vastly different things to say. An SNCC worker said spring in Lowndes County, Alabama, is "cotton-picking hell." It is a world unknown to Keats. One student said what seems difficult for so many white people in America to understand: we as black people must have the power to write about *what is ours and ours alone*—when we can do this "we know we are alive."

Tuskegee: an affluent black community. Many faculty and employees have built homes around the school; the Institute has established itself as a community in its own right. Small picturesque lake, good fishing, excellent farming—not difficult to see how Booker T. Washington's philosophy became rooted in agriculture and labor. Or to understand the rationale behind Carver's experiments with soil. The veterinary medicine school and Carver Experimental Laboratory are still thriving and, I understand, highly respected.

The statue of Booker T. "lifting the veil of ignorance" is interesting. If you look at it closely there seems to be some question whether he is lifting the veil or placing it on. At the Dorothy Hall restaurant, waiters affect a demeanor which might be the final culmination of Washington's teachings. Marvelous Kentucky bourbon black waiter manners.

Tonight, reading from his own poetry, David Henderson added something unique to our repertory and to the experience of the Tuskegee audience. His poems—personal, mystical, urban—are not the type Negro college students have been exposed to, but David hypnotized the audience. He responded to questions about his work for almost an hour after the reading, then read some more.

July 15—Albany, Georgia

We left Tuskegee late, as usual, for Albany, Ga., where we will be for two days on the last leg of this tour. It was a beautiful drive from Tuskegee through rich Alabama and Georgia country, through "Terrible Terrell" County; through red clay, red hills, and ramshackle shacks where, as in Mississippi, black people always live by the roads and the tracks. While we sped in convoy toward Albany we listened on the radio to the Senate hearing on Mississippi poverty. Senator Eastland: "Why, Ah've known the Nigras all my life. Nothing could be further from the truth than that we want to starve them out. Why, if they all left, I'd go with them. I know all the Nigras in these counties personally."

He is talking about the Mississippi Delta, about Sunflower County, where we had been three months ago to play for people with an average income of $650 per year. We haven't come so far since then—Texas to Georgia with the Mississippi Delta in the center: all variations on the same theme. Georgia red clay and Georgia shacks roll by. We stop for gas at a general store, take some pictures. Things haven't changed much in a hundred years. Back on the road more news informs us of the growing war in Newark. Fourteen black people dead. Poet LeRoi Jones arrested and beaten. The cat on the news wants to know "where will it all end."

When we arrived in Albany we discovered that Bob had made arrangements for us to play in Sylvester, about thirty miles away. We performed the poetry show in a small church on a dusty road off the main highway, at the annual meeting of the Worth County Improvement League. It was an inspiring meeting with strong speeches about pride and determination despite the prices on a few heads in the group. One man said a white man (who considered himself a friend) told him, "Your number is up. The only reason you talkin' to me now is because nobody showed yet to claim your price." After the meeting there was watermelon for everyone and the meeting of new friends.

Outside, beside the church on this clear, scorching Georgia day, was a graveyard, with gravestones dating back to the nineteenth century; Georgia Brown—died June 24, 1965—age 95 years.

Tonight we stay together in the Albany Community House. In the rush and pressure of the tour we see each other all the time but hardly have time to really talk. For once, tonight, we had a groovy, relaxed time together. Carmel Collins cooked marvelous red beans, Murray and Gary made steak. David turned everyone on with his Sun Ra and LeRoi Jones records. Later we ate sliced watermelon and peaches. Tomorrow will be Sunday . . . one more show, one more performance of *Happy Ending*, then we will return to New Orleans. Tomorrow Albany, Ga., will be beautiful and sleepy and we will leave it asleep. With all our crises and disputes we can hardly believe we made it this far. Someday the FST will be everything we want it to be: disciplined and smooth-running; a source of genius and black cultural history. Tonight it is enough that we are (with no one saying it) somewhat marveling at ourselves; we have survived.

Part Six

ROOTS AND EPILOGUES

MOTION IN THE OCEAN:
Some Political Dimensions of the Free Southern Theater

It's not the size of the ship
that makes the waves
It's the motion of the ocean.*

I.

I remember thinking it strange, when I first started working in the Southern Student Movement in 1962, that there were so many people who, like myself, thought of themselves as poets. I wrote a letter (to someone) describing them, us, as poets who had come to the conclusion that the most profound poetry is the poetry of action and movement. When the problem becomes unspeakable then there is simply nothing to say—something must be done.

I was in the third wave of "students" who swept through the South with a dream in the early sixties. Sit-ins in '60, Freedom Rides in '61, and in '62 the forces gathered around the right to vote. After each wave there was a period of uncertainty while the new motion was in the making. That was a time to survey the damage and chaos which often seems to follow in the wake of dreams.

It was that crisp time, October in Mississippi, that quiet shifting time after the summer of '62 on the small storybook campus

* From a prose poem by Charlie Cobb, who credits an Atlanta DeeJay. Ain't no telling where he got it from.

of Tougaloo College near Jackson. I'd heard a lot about Gilbert from others who knew of my interest in theater. They talked about "the black guy who works for the *Free Press* and was in a Broadway show!" (From Mississippi, New York is New York and an Off-Broadway is no less than a Broadway show.) But here at last I had found him, camera in hand, gold-rimmed glasses perpetually sliding off the end of his nose, Gilbert Moses III on his way to the Tougaloo theater to take pictures of the rehearsal of the current student production of *Inherit the Wind* for the newspaper.

After peremptory introductions he indicated his haste to get to his business so I promptly invited myself along. Before long we were talking about theater. Almost immediately the conflict began. The tragic drama, I said, in response to some question or comment, is the highest and most noble of all art forms! Absurd, was his curt reply, anyone who could say that seriously must be both presumptuous and ignorant of the theater. Comedy is the most perfect form, he insisted. We talked on, it seemed, till dawn. Later that week I moved into Gilbert's apartment, as I was just returning to Jackson and needed a place to live. That was the beginning of the dialogue that led to the birth of the Free Southern Theater.

Each of us had come to the South with the naïve thought that it would not take more than a few years to do what we had come to do there before going on with our lives. Each of us came to realize after a short time that it was not a matter of a few years, work by a few people, that would be required. We would have to spend lifetimes in the faith that a few keys might be found if enough people worked long enough and hard enough.

We both felt bound in the apparent contradiction between the poet and the person. We claimed to be playwrights and poets; yet the political facts of life presented by the situation we first learned of in the South called for a life of useful, political or economic, engagement. How could we remain true to ourselves and our own concerns as artists and at the same time remain true to our developing recognition of what might be called a political responsibility?

There was another person, Doris Derby, a young black painter from New York. She pointed the way to resolution in a conversation one day. "If theater means anything anywhere, it certainly ought to mean something here!" That was the magic chord.

Since then the FST has been more about struggle than realization. Work, people, time, money and philosophy—incessant philosophy! Where to find good people who could stand the pressure of time and working in a hostile environment. Always feeling the pressure of time—the need to do more, be in more places, to do more plays, talk to more of "the people"! Never knowing whether there will be enough money for the next week's payroll or to repair the truck the next time it breaks down and some damn fool agent sends in a bill for royalties on a script and threatens legal action if we don't pay. Arriving in Clarksdale to find all our posters and publicity material never got off somebody's desk and no arrangements were made for us to have a place to stay, or food, and the minister of the church expects rent for the three or four days we'll be using his church—actors on the streets with handbills, going from door to door, "A real live play—tomorrow night! . . ."

The disappointment of the discovery that the big benefit only made $2,000, not enough to get us to the end of the month. The hassles that grew from the barrier that isolated the whites involved from the blacks in the company, and the difficulty of making that connection with the audience. Perhaps the most dreadful struggle of all, the one to keep up that energy required to go on in the drab fashion afforded by the *real* situation, while being tortured by the vast, almost overwhelming, potential implicit in the idea. The constant struggle against the confusion engendered by racism internally and externally—in the theater and out of it, within the black community and out of it. And finally, as if we didn't have enough problems, the constant struggle with those who felt that our theater was either *too* political or *not political enough.* That political question—the relationship between politics and art; between what we and our peers in the "Movement" were doing—consumed the largest part of the philosophical struggle.

Those philosophical expressions in and around the FST have brought me to some working conclusions which now operate as keys to my own perspective, and which summarize the effect of that continuing dialogue on me.

There is a popular tendency to separate politics and art, much the way the church and state are separated, which strikes me as being improperly conceived. We learn in schools that politics is one thing and art is another and that it is not valid to be both at the same time. But that is a false dichotomy.

We talked a lot about the relationship between art and politics, and found ourselves saying the same thing over and over again. It is finally a relationship in the abstract. A man simply cannot be divided like that. As a matter of essential form, the theater, all the arts in fact, are political. The question is whose political interests will a particular theater or a particular production serve.

The artist, to grow, must be nurtured by those who love him. If he loves not wisely, then his love devours him. If his love is wise, then all love's the better for it. It seems simple, then, to make a place for black artists to be with people who love and can nurture them. When the black artist speaks to a critical audience that is not also black, he speaks from one set of cultural and political interests and experience to an audience with different, sometimes hostile priorities and contradicting experience. The black artist, in order to communicate across that gap, becomes an *explainer.* He must interpret how his own experience relates to the "human experience" of white people so they can understand it. His time is spent in pursuit of more effective explanations of characters or images. That process takes him away from his legitimate work as an artist. One may be eversogood a poet, in one's heart, but to explain a rose rather than to sing is not to make a poem, but an explanation of a rose—in verse perhaps, but an explanation nonetheless. It is the poet's task to sing.

The black artist suffers from the white audience because he must speak from a divided consciousness to a mentality that refuses to acknowledge the most essential part of that consciousness. He is further limited by institutionalized forms that incorporate or presume the premises of racism—cultural, political, and economic institutions. He is bound by a series of contradictions at the outset if his *intended* audience (the frame of reference) is white. Few are those who have found the means to transcend those contradictions while remaining vital as artists and "successful" in the established terms.

The more seriously the black artist tries to affect the white consciousness, the more explicative he must become. The more explicative he becomes, the less attention he gives to the essentials of his art. A kind of negative value field is established. Racism systematically verifies itself when the slave can only break free by imitating the master: by contradicting his own reality.

As long as the victims of racism accept the judgments of their oppressors and rely on the approbation of that society, they are locked in. If they do not recognize the presence of positive standards and values in the black community, then they love unwisely, and will be devoured by their own flames. When the positive connection is made the world opens up and creativity blooms. The question is not whether or not the black community has standards and values of artistic importance, but whether the black artist will accept the responsibility of speaking within the context of and to those values and needs.

The presumed antipathy between politics and economics on the one hand, and art and culture on the other, could better be described as an antipathy between politicians and artists. Because of the strength of the Western political establishment the schism between artists and politicians has been institutionalized, in order to defend the establishment against a growing list of contradictions in Western culture that have developed out of the efforts of that culture to survive as king of the volcano when the time for playing that game is gone.

II.

The real question, how to be relevant to the lives of our audience, was one that couldn't be handled abstractly. The theater, as a discreet form, is largely foreign to the cultural experience and heritage of the black audience.

Some generalities seemed pretty clear: The lack of money should not keep people away from the theater. Most of the people we were most concerned about have very little if any money. We therefore concluded that the theater was to be free. Our plays, to be relevant, had to connect with the life. In a real sense, those plays have not been written yet. Those who live the life must write the particular truth of their experience.

So the objective became clear: To make the form, theater, available to the black people in the South with the expectation of making the form integral to the cultural experience.

It would not be enough simply to perform. We felt the need for a way to really get *involved* with and to involve and interest the residents of local communities. The touring company, no matter how relevant, stimulating, or exciting in a given repertoire, could not speak to the continuing need of people wanting deeper involvement. The Community Workshop Program, an ongoing, year-round program geared specifically to the participation of local people, was developed to meet this need. (Lack of funds for this program has made it impossible to extend it outside New Orleans at the time of writing. Indeed, funding is a continual threat to the whole operation!)

Since a theater of the black people of the South must ultimately be made of those people, the task of the touring company, which is largely "imported," is in one sense to catalyze the involvement of local people in the workshop program. The forms, techniques, and even the aspirations of the people we spirit off to the South are by and large defined by the established theater, movies, and television. The culture that produces those forms is different from and has only an abstract relationship to the culture and environment of Southern blacks. We speak a language and a line with forms of our own. That culture produces its own definition and relevance.

Relevance in the theater finally depends on the plays. While there is a sense in which all good plays (art) are universal, therefore relevant to all human experience, each of us finds most full that particular reflection of ourselves and our own experience. There is a dreadful scarcity of plays that grow out of and reflect the experience of black people in this country. The reason, I think, lies in the absence of enough theaters in which black writers can develop. The theaters that do exist will remain more potential than real until the form itself is seen in the black community as a meaningful and useful vehicle for the expression and clarification of experience. There are some plays by and about Negroes. But of those that were not written by whites, the majority were written with the presupposition of a white audience and from that base of values. The process of making form and sense to the black community cannot bypass the kind of involvement we seek in the Community Workshop Program.

Our search for relevant scripts has led into all kinds of political problems. One fellow who was in our company for a time was refused his petition for conscientious objector status by his draft board because he was working for the FST during the 1965 season, which we called "The Year of Revolt." That bill included *Shadow of a Gunman* by Sean O'Casey, *The Rifles of Senora Carrar* by Brecht, and *In White America* by Martin Duberman. The fact that we would produce such a bill was taken as evidence of our "support of violence" and therefore invalidated his claim.

The plays chosen for "The Year of Revolt" did not aggravate our cohorts in the South. Those connections seemed clear.

Our production of *Waiting for Godot,* on the other hand, irritated the hell out of people.

Time and time again, the question was raised, "What possible relevance do you imagine *Godot* to have to the lives of black people in the South?" One of the most common arguments against the play was that it was too "complicated and intellectual" for the "ignorant rural mind." Not only is this a condescending and patronizing argument, it is one symptomatic of misplaced Western values which presume education as a prerequisite for intelligence. The uneducated may lack certain specific skills that follow education but they are no less intelligent. Often the very absence of those skills forces people to a greater application of creative facilities simply in order to survive in competition in a system loaded against those specific deficiences.

Moreover, theater is a living art. While the script is important, the immediate communication takes place between the actors on stage and the audience. The audience is confronted with a theatrical, not a literary, experience. Our production of the play was very good and did, therefore, communicate forcefully.

Some saw it as a political allegory. Mrs. Fannie Lou Hamer in Ruleville, Mississippi, best typified that approach when she said in the discussion after the play, "Every day we see men dressed just like these (tramps), sitting around the bars, pool halls, and on the street corners waiting for something! They must be waiting for Godot! But you can't sit around waiting. Ain't nobody going to bring you nothing. You got to get up and fight for what you want. Some people are sitting around waiting for somebody to bring in Freedom just like these men are sitting here. Waiting for Godot . . ."

Others read it as a religious allegory making Godot God and the central image the fall of man in the second act. Ultimately,

I think it must be agreed that *Godot*, although a brilliant theater piece, is not the most appropriate kind of material.

It surprised me to notice, after the theater moved from Jackson to New Orleans, in 1964, how much we were dependent on Movement activity. The theater depends on its relationship to the activists for relevance and perspective. The awareness of that activity is extremely important for the orientation of people who have not previously been engaged, and the dialogue is important to all. On our arrival in New Orleans, we felt less relevant because there was very little Movement activity going on in the city. Since that time things have begun to change; several programs and organizations have emerged. The presence and activity of the FST I think has been a little bit responsible for that.

The relationship between the FST and Movement people is important also because it opens up the question of the arts as propaganda. It is important to distinguish between the inevitable political function of the arts and propaganda. Propaganda is a legitimate and necessary function of partisans to a political viewpoint. The artist has license not available to the propagandist, however. A given work of art may have qualities of propaganda, if a given partisan position is made clear or illuminated by the artist's work. But the propagandist has the additional responsibility of shaping information to meet the needs of priorities established by a particular political program.

It is possible to have good propaganda and not have art at all. At the same time, the artist can speak quite sharply to a specific political situation without the sacrifice of art. The artist operates at the vanguard of man's cultural consciousness. In that role his responsibility becomes to inform men's judgments. From this principle derives the aesthetic license. Dereliction of the duty to inform judgment deprives the artist of relevance and leaves him defenseless against history's indictment. Propaganda, on the other hand, demands an absolute certainty, a line for which the artist can be held responsible.

In a similar way the (commercial) entertainment theater business is not relevant to the development of a black theater. Nonetheless, most of the black artists have been taken away from the cultural basis of their own development by the lure of "success." Only recently, since the shift in political circumstances has pulled the blacks into center-stage, has it become possible for the commercial black artist to retain a bit of integrity without jeopardizing his commercial option too seriously. Even so, the fact that most of the commercial markets include blacks to no significant degree makes those markets largely irrelevant to us.

In the creation of a relevant theater the development of an active rather than a passive audience—a critical audience—is the most important task. It is not enough that a particular theater group be composed of black people or even that it be located physically in a place where black people live. To a very great extent, these two points are not important if the theater is not addressed to the needs of black people and grounded in the context of that experience. "Exposure" is not only a patronizing concept, it does not develop an audience critical and reflective to its own needs. Being in Ireland is not what made the Irish theater Irish, it was the positive search for the theatrical forms which comprehend and speak to that ineluctably Irish soul. When one finds the essence of an Irishman one finds the same truth that binds all men. Yet the statement remains distinctively Irish. And so with any culture.

If an "Irish" theater could be distinguished from an English theater only because it had Irishmen and was in Ireland, then it would be an English theater in Ireland. The distinction is largely political. A theater run and operated by Negroes, that can be distinguished from other theater in this country only by the complexion of the cast, is not a black theater; it is a white theater with Negroes.

The inescapable fact of the matter remains. There is no truth that speaks so clearly to me as the truth of my own experience.

If I cut to the essence of my own truth there will lie a truth for all men. One can only achieve that kind of statement, however, in the context of specific historical, cultural, political, economic circumstances. One's work, regardless of whether one deals directly with those concepts or not, must be done with a comprehension of these problems.

As the truth of black people finds expression in theatrical forms, new forms will be created. As that truth finds expression, it will be political. It will be opposed to the ruling powers because history, and the ruling powers, make it so. The Free Southern Theater is one part of the process in the larger context of that struggle.

It's not the ship
that makes the waves
It's the motion of the ocean.

A Chapter in the Etymology of the Word Negro

In the winter of 1965–1966 I did play research for the Free Southern Theater while semi-vacationing in New York City. I set about the very dusty task of reading daily in the Schomberg Collection of the New York Public Library and the very dirty one of rampaging about the city looking for little books of plays from Africa. One day, while drowsing in the library over notes and a book called something like *They Shall Not Die,* I noticed sitting across the hardwood table a clean-shaven (head), clean-cut young black cat devouring a thin but obviously absorbing volume called something like *A History of the Moors in Spain or Spanish History from 1000 A.D. to 1300 A.D.* I became curious about the fellow because I noticed him eyeing me periodically over either the top or the side of his little book. Shortly, I took a break for a cigarette in the front hallway of the library, which faces onto 135th Street. My ready friend followed. We engaged each other in conversation very quickly, and I soon found myself very quietly listening to a flow of quoted history and an analysis of the word "Negro" as it has been used down the centuries by various groups (most of them not Negro at all). When the fast-flowing, highly enthusiastic lecture was over, I asked him for what good reason he was spending so much time finding out about one little good-for-nothing word. He then told me of his Muslim affiliation, and his attempts to rediscover history from a black point of view. Having read a little about the Muslims, and having been in the South for the previous year and a half, and having begun to develop, as a consequence, a view of things quite different from the one I'd been taught in most of the all-white schools I'd attended, I wasn't surprised at his diligence and determination. My friend awakened some slow-burning coals in my soul, brought into clear focus some ideas that my husband Gil Moses and I and other black members of the Free Southern Theater had touched on at various times but had not really seriously thought about. When I left the library that day I headed straight for Micheaux' book store and bought some things I'd kept forgetting to pick up—excerpts from Malcolm's speeches (we already had the autobiography) and Frantz Fanon.

But more important than the books I bought that day, or any other day, I left that library feeling for the first time that something was beginning to glue black people back together again. Something simple, and I guess profound, an inkling of unity. I call that winter, that anniversary of Malcolm's death, my first rebirth. Some of us call it "instant" blackness; but when I think about it, that's hanging a pejorative tag on something that is very real, and very valuable. I don't think when it comes, it's a sign that you should throw your brain and your rationality in the river; it's just consciousness, touch, awareness—of some things that have always been there and that something is dreadfully out of kilter. It's something like living with someone for years without knowing how much you despise him, and then one word, one gesture and the you-know-what hits the fan.

We're strong on the wrong kinds of traditions and myths in this country, and fast, trigger-sharp changes are common.

As I boarded the subway train to go home that evening, I noticed a black girl with natural hair. My hair is straight for the most part and when I was growing up I never felt that particular pang about not having straight hair like all the pretty white girls had. My folks flaunted my "gift" for me constantly. Not everyone in my family has straight hair. I was taught fairly early how to "do" hair because my grandmother, who lived with us, had arthritis in her hands and couldn't afford the beauty shop. I used to straighten her hair, following her directions meticulously. I only burned her on the nape of the neck, or on the ear, once or twice. So obviously this girl, with her hair, says, "I'm not going to try to look like you any more because I've got something equally beautiful." And what can you say to that but Amen?

As the days passed in New York, I noticed more and more "natural" heads, though not by any means enough, and noticed more interest in black music, books, poetry, history, African cultures. And I felt in my soul that we were the chosen people, and could make that felt if only we had a leader. I read and listened and looked, and I felt black, completely, for the first time in my life. (Being "light brown skinned" I've had to fight doubly hard at times since to be anointed "black," but I've relaxed with my whereabouts and whatabouts now and it's not nearly so important to me in my everyday life. I am what I am, obviously a hybrid as are most blacks in this country. It doesn't trouble me any more because in itself it is unique and full of potential.)

So, back to the South we went, Gil and I, to begin again the project Free Southern Theater. I remember, en route to New Orleans, vivid, hearty conversations about Fanon, Black Power, Black Theater. Talk about black women seemed always to be particularly energetic. We gave a lift to some Snicks in Alabama and the conversation got livelier still. Gil and I were getting all our rationales into a proposal for an all-black theater and preparing to present it to the integrated Board of Directors of FST. We not only wanted to have an all-Negro theater—people in the South are very used to all-black everything; the idea wasn't so new in that sense—but we thought a definite political and aesthetic change of program was needed, one which would help us to get a few of the basic things we had always wanted for the Free Southern Theater—a Negro face, a Negro art, a Negro idea. So we pushed and shoved and fought and talked and met with resistances we never even imagined would be alive.

We never got a black theater but we at least got people to see that a 9/10ths black theater was all we would accept. Gil left in the midst of the turmoil, and some few of us stayed on to try to finish the season, which we hadn't really been able to get started for the political haranguing—all of which was necessary and tolerated, because we were not politically or artistically secure enough to accept the oneness of our art and our politics.

We eventually settled down to working on three wonderful short shows which were fun to do and tremendously exciting for the audiences. But I was in love with Africa—the idea of Africa, the blackness of Africa, the home Africa—and full of who I was, and the world was coming into icy focus.

One of the plays we did that season was Gil's *Roots*. While I was rehearsing Dot, my mind was filled with fantasies of a flood of black people all at the same point—ready to *take* what had been denied for so long, ready to weld together and use our numbers as a club in the political arena with such political suavity and acumen that in no time flat we'd be together, ready to grab hold of our past, our present, and our future and shimmy it in Whitey's face. I wanted to contribute. I wanted to see little children walk with their heads high, reading Negro history, understanding fully this bind Whitey put us in. So, having collected a minimum of materials and made some few contacts, I set about writing up a proposal for the founding of an Afro-American/African Information Center at our building in the Ninth Ward of New Orleans. And I had the technical director build shelves, and I put in the few things I had, and I worked out a cataloguing system. I began gathering small groups of youngsters in the hot early afternoon sun to read and look at pictures from Africa and other parts of the world.

Denise Nicholas

ROOTS

by Gilbert Moses

An old Negro couple, to be played by young actors. Dinner time. In a dining room of the utmost poverty. Windows with plastic over them; table dirty, peeling paint. A barrel for one seat, a rickety chair for the other. A Coke bottle with cotton sticking out of it for floral decoration. The couple is dressed in rags, from feet to head. It is cold. A pot-belly stove. There is a statue of Jesus Christ hanging on the wall. A calendar with a white girl on it, etc.

Lights up on woman in the kitchen, cooking. She wears a gas mask, which she intermittently raises to her forehead, then goes to the window to get a sniff of fresh air, then returns to the cooking.

Husband enters. He has a gigantic cotton bag hanging from his shoulders. He looks to see if Dot can see him, then starts to go off-stage. He goes back inside the house.

DOT Did you wash everything?

RAY Yes. (RAY *is rather nervous, carries paper in his hand.*)

DOT You're becoming so absent-minded in your old age. Did you wash your ears?

RAY Yes.

DOT Are you sure?

RAY I washed up, Dot.

DOT All right, now. Don't let me find out you haven't. I'll send you right outside. (RAY *stands, hesitant.*)

RAY Dot? Can I sit down?

DOT Sho, you can sit down. (RAY *starts to move.*) If you've washed up.

RAY I washed up, Dot.

DOT All right, then you can sit down. (RAY *sits at dining table, starts to drum his fingers on the table, on glasses. He is a man who makes music out of anything. He uses silverware, the metal parts of his suspenders. Starts to sing, "Ohhhhh, me. Ohhhhhhh me," in traditional blues style. He leans back on chair beginning to stomp his feet.*)

DOT Ray? Don't bring that noise in here. . . . Raymond?

RAY Huh?

DOT You better take that noise out of here. (RAY *stops, embarrassed. He starts quickly to read newspaper.* DOT *has jar of preserves in her hand.*)

DOT Why are you reading the newspaper without waiting on me?

RAY There's no harm in it, Dot.

DOT It makes me feel funny.

RAY There's no harm in it, Dot. I can't read.

DOT I know. That's why it hurts me so when you come in and sit down and start to read. You can't read.

RAY I know, Dot.

DOT Well, why don't you wait for me then? I'm your wife.

RAY I know, Dot.

DOT I work to fix you a good dinner. I get you everything you want, so why don't you wait for me?

RAY I'm just looking at it, Dot.

DOT But you can't read. You know that.

RAY I'm just looking at it, Dot. (DOT *hands him jar of preserves.*)

DOT Here. Open this.

RAY (*Tries*) Ohhhhh. I can't.

DOT Hand it over. (*She opens it easily.*) Hmmmmmmmmph!

RAY I'm not as strong as I used to be.

DOT Your coffee.

RAY I need something hot. I'm very cold.

DOT It's warm coffee.

RAY I'm not so hot over warm coffee, Dot.

DOT You like your coffee hot, tasting like melted nuts, huh?

RAY I like that, Dot.

DOT Well, I don't have enough pots.

RAY But I'm an old man, Dot. I need something hot.

DOT Go and drink the stove.

RAY What was that, Dot?

DOT I said, go and drink the stove if you need something hot.

RAY That's very funny, Dot.

DOT I know.

RAY Thanks for the warm coffee, Dot.

DOT You're welcome. (RAY *tastes coffee. He starts to sing softly, patting his feet softly. "Ohhhhhh, ohhhhhhh me."* DOT *looks at* RAY.)

RAY (*To the audience*). I'm an old Negro man. I'm just beginning to sit down to my usual supper of hog maws, navy beans, cornbread, greens, and buttermilk. It's going to be delicious. I've sat down at my usual dinner for forty-five years and I've never wanted nothing else. Because-what-I-eat-is-very-good-and-filling-for-an-old-Negro-man.

Every evening at 6 o'clock, I come home from work to my usual and good supper. I work in the cotton fields. I get two dollars a day. I've been working in the cotton fields ever since I was high enough to reach down and pick. It is hard work for an old Negro man, but I wasn't always this old.

The woman I've been talking to these last forty-five years is my wife, Dot. Dorothea May. She's an old Negro woman—

DOT But I'm a very light-complected Negro woman, Ray.

RAY I know, Dot.

DOT The closest you could come to white.

RAY She's a very light-skinned Negro, with bitsy breasts.

DOT You shouldn't say that, Ray.

RAY It's the truth, Dot.

DOT I know, but you shouldn't say it. It hurts me.

RAY I'm sorry, Dot.

DOT I'd think you'd be tired of hurting me by now.

RAY I'm sorry, Dot. Her breasts don't make me angry. Just sad. She can read. And she has a good deal of education, which I don't. She went as far as the eighth grade. She comes from a good light-skinned family, which I don't. We have no children, because Dot, she feels—

DOT Don't say that, Ray.

RAY Why not, Dot? It's the truth.

DOT I know. But it hurts. It's God's fault, not mine.

RAY Because of God. But that don't bother me, it just makes me feel funny. Especially when I see all the other families with ten and twelve children, working in the cotton fields with them. I've always wanted a little boy to hand my cotton to. Sometimes in the fields I turn around to hand my cotton to my little boy and there's no one there. And I feel a little funny.

We've lived in the South for a long time, ever since we were born. Except Dot.

DOT Oh, Ray. You don't have to mention that.

RAY Except Dot. She worked out of the South for a while.

DOT (*Flattered*) I used to be a maid in Maryland. But that was nothing.

RAY Ain't that still the South, Dot?

DOT Well, so is New York.

RAY I've never been to New York.

DOT And you've never been to Maryland neither.

RAY I know, Dot.

DOT So you wouldn't know. Maryland is out of the South.

RAY She worked out of the South for a while.

DOT (*Flattered*) I was a maid for some rich white folks in Maryland. But that was nothing.

RAY But she came back here. We don't like it here. But we can't leave. So we like it pretty good. Dot takes care of our house just like she takes care of the white folks' house. Which is better than some people who don't have no houses to take care of at all. We have a bedroom, an outhouse, and a kitchen that's the dining room too.

DOT It's bigger than what most people got, Ray.

RAY I'm proud of it, Dot.

DOT It's no shotgun house.

RAY Sho' ain't.

DOT Most people have shotgun houses.

RAY I'm proud of it, Dot. It's a good house for an old Negro man who has a light-complected-skin wife. I come home to my castle every evening.

DOT But you don't stay home.

RAY Sometimes I shoot a little crap with the boys.

DOT (*To the audience*) Every night.

RAY A man has to take a stretch sometimes, Dot.

DOT Not every night.

RAY I love to shoot crap, Dot.

DOT (*To the audience*) Not every night. I don't care, of course. He might as well stay home. He thinks going next door is taking a stretch. This man has made a rut from the cotton patch to this house to next door. I don't think he's been further than that in his life. But that's just like an old Negro man.

RAY I come home to my bony castle and Dot says to me . . .

DOT Have you washed? Everything?

RAY And I say, yes. And she says . . .

DOT You're becoming so absent-minded in your old age. Did you wash your ears?

RAY And I say, yes.

DOT Are you sure?

RAY I washed up, Dot. (DOT *takes the newspaper and starts to read.*)

DOT Monday, December 3rd, 1965.

RAY Today is Friday, Dot.

DOT It says right here Monday, December 3rd, 1965.

RAY Funny, Dot. It's Friday.

DOT It says right here, Monday.

RAY Funny . . .

DOT Weather report: clear and sunny.

RAY That must be wrong. I'm freezing, Dot.

DOT It says right here. Weather report: clear and sunny.

RAY But it's very cold.

DOT Only to you. To other people it's clear and sunny. Isn't that nice?

RAY But I'm freezing, Dot.

DOT But others aren't. Everybody else is feeling clear and sunny.

RAY I'm glad to hear it.

DOT I don't feel very clear and sunny myself.

RAY I'm freezing, Dot.

DOT But it's nice that others are feeling sunny.

RAY Yes. It's real nice.

DOT You know, it's just like you to be freezing when others are feeling clear and sunny.

RAY I can't help it, Dot.

DOT I know you can't help it, but it's just like you anyway.

RAY You said you don't feel too sunny yourself.

DOT That's right. I don't feel too sunny. But anyway, I ain't freezing.

RAY I can't help it, Dot. It's cold.

DOT I know. But it's just like you.

RAY I can't help it, Dot. (DOT *goes on reading the paper.*)

DOT Oh. Oh. Oh. Something awful's happened.

RAY What, Dot? Tell me.

DOT Something awful. (*She avidly reads the paper, making*

sounds softly, and sometimes loudly, to herself as she follows the story.)

RAY What is it, Dot? Oh, tell me. Tell me.

DOT It's really horrible.

RAY What is it, Dot?

DOT (*Reading with her finger*) Fell flat . . . and . . . stairs . . . and . . . Specialist . . . sorry . . . and . . . telegram. Oh, it's just too awful.

RAY Read it to me, Dot. Tell me.

DOT Miss Mississippi has broken her little finger.

RAY Sho nuff?

DOT Hmmmm-hm. Isn't that just awful?

RAY Yes, sure is, Dot.

DOT She hopes that all Mississippians will pray for her.

RAY We sure will, Dot.

DOT They show her picture.

RAY In the hospital?

DOT No. Winning the Miss Mississippi title.

RAY Why don't they show her in the hospital?

DOT It's unbecoming to show young girls in the hospital.

RAY Not if they're sick.

DOT No one wants to look at a pretty young girl who's in the hospital.

RAY If they're sick, Dot . . .

DOT But she just broke her little finger, Ray.

RAY Then why is she on the front page, Dot?

DOT Because she's Miss Mississippi, Ray.

RAY It's sure awful, Dot. (*Pause*)

DOT I could've been Miss Delta.

RAY But you didn't try out, Dot.

DOT I know. But I would have won it, if I had tried out.

RAY Boy. You sure could've.

DOT If I had been Miss Delta, would you've loved me more, Ray?

RAY I loved you all I could, Dot.

DOT But if I'd been Miss Delta, Ray . . .

RAY You didn't try out, Dot.

DOT I probably wouldn't have married you.

RAY I loved you all I could, Dot.

DOT I remember you telling me to try out, Ray, but I was afraid.

RAY I told you to, Dot.

DOT I know. But I was afraid. But I could've won, couldn't I have, Ray?

RAY Boy! You sure could've.

DOT And then I wouldn't have married you.

RAY I would've still loved you, Dot.

DOT I would've been a doctor's wife, or a lawyer's wife, or even a minister's wife.

RAY You could've been anything you wanted to be, Dot.

DOT I know. But I was afraid.

RAY You should've tried out, Dot.

DOT I would have been Queen of the Delta. (*Music: melancholy cello music*) Queen. My arms full of magnolias. I would've strolled, my long white dress flowing, down the cotton-strewn platform. An orchid pinned . . . right here. And I would've strolled . . . People's arms would have reached out to touch me. I'd smile, my radiant smile. Slow down and let them touch my dress. (*She goes through the motions herself, feeling different parts of herself, her clothes.*) Oh. It would be too, too lovely. I'd have my pick. White men would ask to take me out. But I'd blush and say no. Colored men would take me out. I would be the blossom, the sun-colored lily for colored men. I'd just say no to the white men, and give my arm to a Negro doctor, and we'd stroll out of the park. . . . I'd say no. I'm the flower of the Negro world. And everywhere I'd walk, men would tip their hats, kiss my hands. In my yellow dress, frills, strolling down the streets. . . . Oh. It would be too, too lovely. (*Music stops abruptly as if someone has picked up the needle.* DOT *places the gas mask on her face.*) I'd put on a golden veil, my arms full of roses, and stroll down the streets.

RAY That's no veil, Dot.

DOT (*Sadly, knowingly*) I know. (*Pause*)

RAY I loved you all I could, Dot. (*Pause*)

DOT I know. (*She takes off her gas mask.*)

RAY God, Dot.

DOT It's all right, Ray . . .

RAY Goddamn it, Dot.

DOT No use crying about spilt milk, Ray.

RAY (*Is near tears*) God, Goddamn it, Dot.

DOT (*Watches him—goes back to newspaper*). If the front page is that exciting, just imagine what's in the other pages. Oh, my. (RAY *is trying to cry, he perhaps bangs his fists on the table. Trying to cry*)

DOT Stop trying to cry, Ray.

RAY I'm just trying, Dot.

DOT I know. But you know you can't cry.

RAY I was just trying, Dot. (*Silence*)

DOT Would you like your food now?

RAY Yessum.

DOT (*Goes to stove. Brings bowl*) Navy beans.

RAY They look delicious.

DOT (*Repeats stove-bowl action, or plate.*) Greens.

RAY Skunk cabbage . . . smells good.

DOT Cornbread.

RAY Sweetcake. Hoooo, hooooo!

DOT And chitterlings.

RAY No hog maws, Dot?

DOT Chitterlings.

RAY We usually have hog maws, don't we, Dot?

DOT Yeah, well, tonight we have chitterlings.

RAY They smell better than hog maws, Dot.

DOT I still wear the mask, no matter what I cook.

RAY Even when you cook chitterlings, Dot?

DOT No matter what I cook.

RAY Even when you cook steak, Dot?

DOT I cooked steak once. In Maryland.

RAY You didn't wear it then, did you, Dot?

DOT Only when I changed Mister Little Tommie's diapers.

RAY But never in the kitchen?

DOT No. Only when I changed Mister Little Tommie's diapers. Bow your head, Ray. All the way, Ray.

RAY Dot? I want to ask you a question. What if we didn't say the blessing, just once?

DOT Ray? Bow your head.

RAY You and Jesus Christ, Dot. Oughta be one meal, without saying the blessing. Just to see what happens.

DOT Nothin'll happen, Ray. Ain't you thankful that the good Lord is allowing you to eat? You're an old Negro man. You might not be able to eat if not for him.

RAY Hah! As long as my teeth stay put, I'm able to eat all right.

DOT You might not have been able to get out of bed this morning, Ray. Don't you want to thank the good Lord for helping you breathe this morning?

RAY I thank him, Dot. But something's funny. He gives me just enough breath to pick cotton, 'cause after that I ain't got none left.

DOT The Lord works in mysterious ways, Ray.

RAY He sho do!

DOT So now, bow year head, Ray.

RAY Dot. Something's funny. Is Jesus Christ white or does he have a big nose, and, uh, two big feet like I do? Is he black or white?

DOT The Lord ain't got no color, Ray. We all his children.

RAY He got to have some color. Every statue I see of him is white. See. Our picture shows him white.

DOT Stop this foolishness, Ray. Do you think that the good Lord would be black? (*Laughing*) Ohhh, me.

RAY Dot, don't you see?

DOT See what, Ray?

RAY Don't you see, Dot? Something's funny.

DOT I'll say. But I'm asking you. See what, Ray?

RAY Why? Uh, why come? Uh, how for? For why?

DOT Bow your head, Ray.

RAY Yessum. (*He bows his head.*) Oh, Lord. Thank you for letting me get out of bed, for letting me pick cotton, for letting me eat, for letting me be an old Negro man. Humble me, Lord. Sometimes I think I'm being unjustly done in. But humble me, 'cause I can't put my finger on the wrong, Lord. A-men.

DOT That's a good boy, Ray. (*She bows her head.*) Jesus wept.

RAY Awwwww, Jesus. It's terrible here. Terrible! Did you mean it to be this way? And when I die, when I go back to the ashes will I sit on your right hand and know eternal life? Will I? (*A lordly voice on tape:* "Know thy murderers.")

RAY What?

DOT What's wrong, Ray?

RAY What? Why you mysterious S.O.B. If I get there, you better watch out. Because I'll, I'll . . . (*He stands, arm and fist raised to the ceiling.*)

DOT What are you doing, Ray? Who are you talking to, raising your voice like that? (DOT *takes a pie and slams it into* RAY'S *face. What follows is an old-time chase, to be choreographed with fast steps:* RAY *picks up what's left of the pie and smears it on* DOT'S *face.* DOT *bites his finger.* RAY *jumps and howls a little. He goes after her and slips on the floor. He rests. He gets up and chases* DOT *around the table; they wave their arms. They sit at the table and pant for a few seconds.* DOT *says, "You ol' black fool!" The chase continues. He catches her, pretends to hit her with his fist but fools her, and kicks her. She jumps around a bit. She catches him, balls up her fist and trounces* RAY *upon the head, making a hollow sound by popping her cheek with her finger.* RAY *collapses in his chair, breathing hard.* DOT *stands above him, shadow boxing, ready to take him on again, breathing hard.* RAY *whispers feebly, "Uncle."* DOT *like a victorious boxer struts around the table, crying, "I'm the greatest! I am the greatest!"*)

RAY (*Out of breath*) God, Dot.

DOT It's all right, Ray.

RAY Goddamn it, Dot.

DOT Want your buttermilk now?

RAY Yessum. (RAY *begins to crumple his cornbread in his buttermilk.* DOT *quickly puts on sunglasses.*)

RAY I'm finished, Dot.

DOT Did you wipe your hands?

RAY (*He wipes his hands on tablecloth and on underwear.*) I'm finished wiping my hands, Dot.

DOT Are you sure?

RAY Pretty sure, Dot.

DOT All right. (*She takes off sunglasses.*)

DOT You're a sight for two eyes, let alone four.

RAY Why didn't you just close your eyes, Dot?

DOT I closed my eyes once.

RAY Did you?

DOT When I met you.

RAY Awww, Dot . . .

DOT When I was a young girl I used to close my eyes a lot. Ohhhh, I would jump out of bed and squeeze myself and close my eyes. I'd feel myself all over. I couldn't believe it was me. I'd wash up, dress, and eat breakfast and pick up my books to go to school. I went as far as the eighth grade, you know.

RAY I know, Dot.

DOT And the boys would meet me on the way to school and carry my books . . . Even when I didn't go to school, they'd carry my groceries and oh . . . they'd just about do anything for me. But that's not the point. The last time I closed my eyes was to suffocate the only child I ever had.

RAY Because you didn't want it to live, Dot?

DOT Yes, I wanted it to live, Ray.

RAY Then why did you hurt it?

DOT Because it would have been a nigger, Ray.

RAY It might have been a girl.

DOT (*Sighs*) Not much difference.

RAY At least a girl would've been pretty. Like you.

DOT I said I'd never close my eyes again.

RAY Because you hate darkness, Dot ?

DOT Uh huh. It makes me scream. (DOT *shrugs her shoulders. There are no words to explain her emotion.*)

RAY I'm sure enjoying this food. You know, Dot, I'll eat anything you put on the table.

DOT Is it good?

RAY It's what I usually eat.

DOT I know. But is it good?

RAY Oh, Dot, I joined the rabbit club forty-five years ago.

DOT Except there's no lettuce.

RAY There's greens. I joined the LTPC club long time ago too.

DOT The lick-the-plate-clean club? I thought it was the SIUWC club.

RAY That one too. The sop-it-up-with-cornbread club.

DOT The EIAWF club.

RAY The ETPT club.

DOT The CGFIG club.

RAY The belch and fart club.

DOT The ins and outs club.

RAY The ins and outs club?

DOT You know. The interior and exterior club.

RAY I don't remember that one, Dot.

DOT The club that says you cook only the interior: the intestines and the bowels, and the exterior: the snouts, the feet, and the tails.

RAY Oh boy, that's the main club we've belonged to for forty-five years.

DOT We're charter members of the ins and outs club.

RAY That's my favorite club, Dot.

DOT Really?

RAY Well, I don't know if I like it so much.

DOT I don't know if I like it some much either. (DOT *resumes reading newspaper.*)

DOT Oh, listen. McRay is having a zipper sale.

RAY That's one thing we don't need.

DOT I'm glad. They're hard to sew.

RAY Buttons. I only like buttons. I get caught in zippers.

DOT I bet you do.

RAY I only like buttons.

DOT Lemme see. What else? Oh. Allison is selling fur stoles half price.

RAY You won't buy one this week, will you, Dot?

DOT Don't need one yet. I just bought two.

RAY Poor Allison will have to do without us for a while.

DOT What else? Oh. There was an earthquake in Alaska.

RAY A bad one, Dot?

DOT Not too bad.

RAY Are the Eskimos still alive?

DOT It doesn't say.

RAY Those poor Eskimos.

DOT I don't see how they stand it. All that cold.

RAY Me neither.

DOT Business is going up, salons say.

RAY Oh, the salons. The salons. What else do they say?

DOT They congratulate the governor for bringing business into the state.

RAY What business, Dot?

DOT All kind of business. Cotton mills, cottonseed factories, cotton oil refineries, automation, everything.

RAY It's good to be part of the upswing.

DOT Lemme see. That's it.

RAY Read more about the cotton business, Dot. That interests me.

DOT No more about it. (*Lowers the paper*) Ray, why you picking cotton in December?

RAY Huh?

DOT Cotton chopping season is over.

RAY What else can I do?

DOT But cotton chopping season is over. They finished picking last month.

RAY That's a good question, Dot. I guess I'm what they call a cotton picker. In season, out of season. I just picks.

DOT That's just like you.

If the theater can afford it, at this point should come a short silent movie called "Cotton Song." The movie begins with a shot of a cotton field, full of blooming cotton, empty of cotton pickers. The camera closes in on the field, then a row of cotton, and then a single cotton plant. RAY *suddenly jumps out of the cotton—he is hidden until this moment—with bolls in each hand as if he were Zeus with thunderbolts. He smiles. Close-up of serene but beaming face.*

FILM SEQUENCE #*1: During this time, an electric guitarist comes on stage, perhaps a drummer. The music for the film should be supplied by* DOT *and* RAY *and other singers, performing as if they were a down-home rhythm and blues group. If not, then the music should be on tape. The music for Film Sequence* #*2 should be dreamy, serene, gospel music.*

FILM SEQUENCE #*2:* RAY *is picking cotton. He gives the appearance of floating. He picks easily, happily, as if cotton picking were the greatest thing he could do.*

Shot of cotton floating in cotton bag, gracefully.

RAY'S *hands nimbly plucking the cotton.*

Shot of the sun, in morning position.

FILM SEQUENCE #3: *Shot of the sun in midday position.*

Shot of cotton bag with very low level.

RAY *picking cotton furiously, cotton disappearing in bag, but no appreciable change in quantity.*

RAY'S *face—exhaustion.*

We are shown the art of picking, cleaning cotton.

Other workers weighing their bags, talking, laughter.

Women and children just a-pickin'.

A monkey picking cotton.

SOUND: *Rock and roll with work beat.*

FILM SEQUENCE #4: *Sun in evening position.*

RAY *picking furiously. No change in cotton level.*

RAY'S *face—utter exhaustion.*

RAY *as a young man, picking.* DOT *as a young woman brings water.*

RAY *as a middle-aged man, picking.* DOT *as a middle-aged woman brings water.*

RAY *as an old man, picking.*

Different shots of hands picking cotton, different faces. Speed up film. Shot from inside bag. Screen covered with cotton.

RAY, *lying on top of cotton pile.*

RAY, *bursting through wall of cotton.*

Shot of men going home.

Mississippi houses.

Shot of morning sun.

Run film of men going home backwards.

RAY, *dreamily picking cotton in morning sun.*

SOUND: *Blues.*

This is only the framework of a short film, to be worked out in detail by the director. The end result should be cotton saturation, and an awareness of how back-breaking cotton working is. The music sung and played should be as sticky and funky as possible. The film and sound can be omitted. The play flows on without the imposition.

The guitarist and drummer, without pretense, leave set. (DOT *and* RAY *resume dialogue.*)

DOT It's time now, ain't it, Ray?

RAY Not now, Dot. Let's save the good things for last.

DOT We always do that, and never get to it.

RAY Well, wait a minute. Let me reflect a bit on the cotton business.

DOT Reflect on the cotton business. Well, I never . . . (RAY *reflects a bit.*)

RAY Boll weevil. That damn boll weevil spoils everything.

DOT Now you are finished reflecting, I'll turn to it.

RAY Awwww, Dot. Let me finish my chitterlings first.

DOT Ray. You can't run away from everything. At this rate we'll never get to it.

RAY You know, chitterlings is good to the last greasy gut.

DOT Never eat the things myself. I'm going to turn to it now, Ray.

RAY Read a few more things first, Dot.

DOT There's nothing here, Ray.

RAY There's gotta be more, Dot. It wasn't as good as before.

DOT There's nothing here, Ray.

RAY There's gotta be more, before you turn to it, Dot. We were just getting into it!

DOT Look at you. Blubbering and slobbering. Drinking the cold air in gulps.

RAY I'm sorry, Dot. But shouldn't there be more?

DOT That's all. No more dreams. I'm turning to it now.

RAY Why, Dot? It's for you too.

DOT For me? I don't close my eyes any more.

RAY YOU DON'T HAVE TO CLOSE YOUR EYES, DOT.

DOT You raise your voice one more time and I'll . . .

RAY But Dot . . .

DOT I'll turn to it. I'll turn to NEGRO ACTIVITIES.

RAY (*Whispers*) I'm sorry, Dot.

DOT It's too late to be sorry.

RAY (*Whispering with all his might*) I'm sorry, Dot.

DOT It's over and done now. There . . . Negro Activities.

(DOT *glares at* RAY.)

DOT Oh, look.

RAY (*Defeated*) What, Dot?

DOT Look! A mouse. Argghhh!

RAY Where, Dot?

DOT The stove. There. Argggghhh!

RAY So it is.

DOT Do something, Ray.

RAY If I had a gun I'd shoot it. Ha. Ha.

DOT They're all over. I'm afraid to step in the kitchen.

RAY It's only a mouse, Dot.

DOT They're all over. Why don't you kill it?

RAY I will. It's only a little mouse.

DOT Why don't you set out the rat traps, Ray?

RAY Can't I wait 'til I finish eating, Dot?

DOT I can't bear it another second, Ray.

RAY All right, Dot. (RAY *gets up, exits, re-enters with armload of mouse traps, big and small, some exaggerated.*)

DOT Put one by the stove.

RAY What shall I use for bait, Dot?

DOT Chitterlings.

RAY That won't do it, Dot. They hate chitterlings.

DOT Preserves. (*She takes jar of preserves, spoon, and baits traps as* RAY *places them. She directs the placing of the traps.*)

DOT There. There. There. Here. There.

RAY All this to catch a teensy mouse.

DOT I remember one more.

RAY You can't catch anything in that, Dot. It's too . . .

DOT Get it anyway.

RAY All right. (RAY *exits, and re-enters with a large rat trap. He staggers under its unwieldiness.*)

RAY Where, Dot?

DOT By the door. (RAY *to door,* DOT *baits trap.*)

DOT There.

RAY Too bad nobody comes to visit us.

DOT Why?

RAY They could get caught in the trap. Ha. Ha. (DOT *takes her seat. Prepares to read Negro Activities.*)

RAY That would be too funny for words. Huh, Dot? Suppose ol' Turnbow came over. Blip! Too funny for words. Oh, me.

DOT Sit down, Ray. (*Silence.* RAY *begins to move around.*)

DOT Ray? Why don't you ever want to read Negro Activities? That's what all old Negro men are supposed to read, Ray. You are an old Negro man, you know. (RAY *is moving.*)

DOT Sit down, Ray. (RAY *hesitates, then sits. Starts to drum his fingers, make music, again.*)

RAY Dot? I'm going to take a stretch.

DOT All right. (RAY *doesn't move. Drums fingers.*)

DOT You can't sit still for one second, can you? (RAY *gets up. Puts on coat, hat, etc. Prepares to leave. He stands in the middle of the room.*)

DOT Sit down, Ray.

RAY (*Quietly*) I'm too damn tired, Dot.

DOT You can't be too tired to sit down, Ray.

RAY I'm damned tired, Dot. Sick and tired.

DOT Well then, take the load off your feet.

RAY (*Mumbling, hesitantly*) I . . . I . . . I . . .

DOT What's gotten into you, Ray?

RAY Ohhh, Dot. Ohhh, Dot. (RAY *moves around the room unsure of where to go. He is afraid.*)

DOT What has gotten into you, Raymond?

RAY (*Not commanding*) Read Negro Activities, Dot.

DOT I'll read it, Ray.

RAY READ NEGRO ACTIVITIES, Dot!

DOT I can't for the life of me understand what's wrong with you, Ray.

RAY READ IT! READ IT! READ IT! (RAY *finds a pair of earmuffs and puts them on.*)

DOT All right, Ray. (DOT *begins to read.*) James Spenders died last week. He was respected by all. Had a large funeral with lots of flowers and Cadillacs. His casket broke the straps and fell into the grave hole. . . . Spenders was a big man in the community. . . . The Greefond Debutantes had a big ball. It lists the names of the people present: Mr. and Mrs. Jones, Mr. Avery the doctor, and his wife, and oh, everybody who's somebody was there. "A gala affair was had by all." (RAY *begins to moan, "Ohhhh me, ohhhhhh me."*) Oh, well! Jimmie Jones got married. What a lovely bride, too. They say it was a beautiful wedding. Ray?

RAY Keep reading, Dot.

DOT Ezekiel Holloway "Lone Dog" Daniels was drafted into the army. Don't he look smart . . .

RAY Not a word.

DOT What's that, Ray?

RAY Not a goddamn word.

DOT There's plenty of words, Ray.

RAY I have questions, Lord, and there's not a goddamn word.

DOT If you took off your earmuffs you could hear better, Ray.

RAY There's . . . nothing . . . when . . . anything . . . something . . . Sometimes I think I'm dying, Dot. I'm dying and I don't even know who I am.

DOT You're an old Negro man, Ray.

RAY You're an old Negro woman.

DOT But very light-skinned.

RAY Anyway, you're old. . . . My feet feel like boulders in the cotton fields.

DOT You shouldn't be ashamed of big feet, Ray.

RAY Nobody's talking about my big feet, Dot.

DOT (*Kindly*) You're an old Negro man, Ray. You can't do nothing. You ain't never done nothing. You ain't got the sense you was born with and you weren't born with nothing. And every day you're getting a little bit older, and you still ain't got nothing.

RAY I know, Dot.

DOT (*Getting stronger*) You could've, if you wanted to, started something out there in that cotton field—a, a, revolution. You could have been bringing home at least five dollars a day. But you didn't.

RAY I know, Dot.

DOT You could have torn down the schools, and the Negro funeral homes, built sewage pipes and sidewalks. You could have taken me away.

DOT You could have given me a child. BUT YOU DIDN'T! (*Silence*)

RAY Dot, I never knew who I was.

DOT So how in hell were you to find out? Asking everybody but yourself.

RAY I'm going out there, Dot.

DOT You might as well sit yourself down. It's too late to do anything now.

RAY I'm going out there, Dot. I've got to! I'll talk it up. I'll . . . DOT! SOMETIMES YOU MAKE ME WANT TO SCREAM!

DOT Go ahead then. Maybe it'll scare all that rotten stuff inside you out. (RAY *walks toward audience. He stops. He tries to scream.* DOT *walks up beside him. Hits him on the back, as if she were burping him. But only once.* RAY *makes a clicking sound as she hits him, but no other sound comes out. He shuts his mouth.* RAY *begins gesturing, as if he's talking to a large crowd.*)

RAY All yawl! Hey, all yawl. You know what I'm talking about and I ain't said nothing. How long . . . how long uh . . . how long . . . (*Pause*) How long can we stay in a strange land without making it our own? . . . Yeah. That's it, ain't it, Dot? . . . All yawl over there, and there, and there. You can't even stand together yourselves, so how we going to do anything together? . . . I going, Dot. . . . Why come we ain't made nothing that looks like us? (RAY *moves around, unsure. He prepares himself to leave, fixing his clothes. He is determined and frantic. He takes a sip of warm coffee. He needs it.*) I HAVE QUESTIONS, LORD! (*He rushes to the door, slips on preserves. There is a loud snap.* RAY *is caught in the rat trap.*)

DOT Ray? Raymond? (RAY *begins to weep. Softly, then building, as lights fade.*) Raymond? It's just like you to be caught in that trap. Just like you. Ohhhh, Lord. You are a sight. Ray? Do you think all old Negro men are like you? I wonder about that sometimes . . . (*Lights fade as* DOT *talks.*)

THE END

The FST and Me

When Gil Moses, John O'Neal, and Doris Derby first wrote to me in February 1964 about the Free Southern Theater, they addressed the letter to "Bill" Schechner. William is my younger brother, a roommate of Gil's at Oberlin, and a newspaperman who worked with the *Mississippi Free Press* in 1963. It wasn't that Gil confused me with Bill. Somehow the slip in addressing me as if I were my brother indicated that the FST people would have preferred my brother. They knew him and they didn't know me. He was their age and I was a few years older. It was easier to deal with Bill than with me.

Ironies always interest me. I accepted the letter for what it was: a strong request for advice coupled with a powerful idea for a theater in the deep South. That this request and idea somehow only accidentally came to me, accidentally not at the business level but at the intention level, remained a quality of my relationship with the FST, and the people who made it what it was and is. At various times during the past five years I have been a producing director, chairman of the Board of Directors, member of the Board, simple adviser, and stage director for the FST. But at no time was I absolutely at the center of the operation. For me, somehow, the FST was an opportunity missed, or not really bull's-eyed. And it is from that slightly off-center position that I can most accurately view the theater and contribute to its progress.

When Gil, John, and Denise Nicholas (later that spring to become Gil's wife, a marriage that lasted a couple of years) arrived at my New Orleans apartment in April, my off-center situation become established. They had come from Jackson, Mississippi, where they were developing the FST from the Tougaloo College Drama Workshop. In New Orleans that week in April was a college theater festival involving all the colleges in New Orleans, including the black ones, Dillard and Xavier. Tulane was the host for the festival, which included performances and discussions. The shows were what one expects from college groups: earnest, intense, sloppy, interesting. The mixture of dialects is something you can only find in the South, where many people have adapted "standard" English, others maintaining their local speech. The variety is not strictly racial, or even regional. It is a class distinction and a revealing one. We all sat in the tiny (168-seat) Tulane University theater and watched the shows. Later we went to my apartment.

My visitors staked out spaces in the living room for the weekend and slept on the couch and on the floor. I lived in those days on St. Charles Avenue, a posh boulevard in the center of uptown New Orleans. (The next fall I was evicted because I had sublet my apartment for two weeks to a black couple. In traditional Southern style, my landlady, who lived below, let me know with superb and offensive tact that her "mother needed the space." It was the first of a series of racial evictions.) We talked about the FST, about how to put a company together, what plays should be done, salaries, touring. We talked about the need for black people in the South to have a theater of their own. But as we talked I realized that I was living on St. Charles Avenue, was a professor, was earning money, taught in a white school. My involvement with Negroes and poor people had not been extensive. I was born in Newark but remember only a few trips with my father into the Negro ghetto. He was a mortgage appraiser and he had to evaluate property. Once he drove into the neighborhood around Springfield Avenue. My mother and I were with him. He got out of the car to look at a building. The neighborhood was dilapidated. I was very young, around ten, and I thought that "good" people would never live in such places. I had an acculturated contempt even for people who lived in two-family houses in my own Weequahic section of Newark. And here, in the ghetto, the houses (there were no "apartments" as I later came to understand that term) were full of hundreds of black people. I could not quite accept them as human, as the same as me. While my father was out of the car a group of kids came running down the block. The car windows were rolled up, it was winter, and they began rocking the car. I was frightened. Soon they left and my father, in his good, heavy coat came back and we drove off. I don't remember speaking to my parents but I do remember that later, when I was in high school, and civil rights (as we called those things then) became important, my mother would argue that Negroes "were inferior" and my father would say that it was all "due to living conditions."

These thoughts come back to me now because I had never "known" black people until I met Gil and John. At college I was involved in some "civil rights" activities and was very much for school integration. I interviewed Thurgood Marshall and wrote some stories about the Supreme Court case for the *Cornell Daily Sun*. Later, as a graduate student, an army private, and an assistant professor I was involved in demonstrations and sit-ins. I was arrested in the New Orleans mayor's office for "refusing to move on" while protesting segregation. But during all that time, black people were "them," citizens whose cause was poignantly just. I was alienated from white culture but could not be part of black culture. There was little personal exchange between me and black people. Most of my friends were white and I felt separated from the very Movement I wished to help because of my whiteness, my Jewishness, and my relative wealth. This situation did not cause me anguish. I accepted it as a matter of course. That was the way the world was. I supported integration, argued for intermarriage as the "final solution," and wanted in the interim total equality: the liberal program.

My entire social view began changing (though perhaps I did not know it at the time) when Gil, John, and Denise stayed at my apartment that week-end in April 1964. They were black and I was white and we were talking. Not simply talking about "the Movement," but about theater, a specific project in which they wanted my collaboration. Over that week-end I decided to join with them and help make the FST a reality. A second meeting was set up in Jackson for early June.

I drove up and went to the apartment John and Gil shared. It was part of a project. Not a new project, but a row of orange-yellow two-story brick buildings. Like so many projects, there was dirt but no lawn, the buildings were in disrepair. There is an important difference between the "rich-poor" (college students scrounging an apartment) and the "poor-poor" (people who have no prospect of living any differently). For the rich-poor there is always a line back to some kind of wealth. Collegetown is an adventure, a tentative step between the security of home and the foreseeable security of a paying job. The poor-poor, however, have children, no clear line to the future, and certainly no past better life willingly renounced. John and Gil were not poor-poor people (they were fresh from college, they were "Movement people," a distinct class in themselves). But they lived among the poor-poor, somewhat in the style of the poor-poor. In short, the ghetto that rocked my father's car when I was ten now became a living reality for me. And for the first time in my life I felt truly out of place. I could speak clearly enough to Gil and John, but to the other people living in the buildings, walking the streets, I wanted nothing more than a nodding acknowledgment. I didn't know what to say to them. Or whether it was necessary for me to say anything.

The three of us met and talked for three days. We rarely left that ground-floor apartment. When we got tired we slept or sat on the front stoop. Gil played the guitar and sang the blues ("Keep on truckin', mama, truckin' all my blues away") and I tried to sing with him. His manner was almost antithetical to John's. John is a slow-talker, a man who develops his thoughts almost painfully, replete with great pauses, excursions, philosophical and religious references. John weaves and works his way through a problem, and his logic is always elegant. Gil is more explosive, moving hurriedly around a space, shooting out remarks, breaking into songs or epithets. John seems peaceful, and Gil constantly at war. The only thing I could talk about to these men was theater. It was the safe middle ground, something that brought us together. And so we talked about it. We wrote a program for the FST. It was not the first and not the last, but it was a succinct statement and I think it still describes the theater's intentions. (See pp. 3–6.) And then, as if we were fully conscious of the "historic moment," we all signed the statement and the FST was officially born. We would start a "professional" theater in the South; we would perform for black audiences in the cities and towns; we would tour; we would train artists. It was a mixture of the Movement, my own ideas about regional theater, and the confrontation among three different personalities.

And it was the first piece of FST rhetoric that I had a hand in proclaiming. It seems now, after these four years, that the FST has always been long on rhetoric, short on achievement. But it is not a simple matter. Not a direct criticism. The early summer of 1964 was the beginning of "Freedom Summer." It sounds like so many years ago! "Black and White Together" was the slogan. Thousands of college kids were streaming into Mississippi to "liberate" that state. Projects were springing up all over the deep South. The FST would participate in that liberation, would add to the political movement its cultural basis; provide a forum for "reflective" thought (John's term, and I'm not sure that any of us knew what it meant, but it sounded *right*). We wanted to organize a company, bring people South, train the people who were already there, and make "a theater for those who have no theater." The rich-poor would speak to, and lead, the poor-poor.

I don't think we should look back on that summer with contempt. Nor should we romanticize it. It was a watershed. At the time we felt that it would be a reservoir of good will, a turning point, a time when blacks and whites together changed the nature of American society. Malcolm X was speaking in the North, the seeds of Watts, Newark, and Detroit were sown long before. But the betrayals to come, the hardships, the unfulfilled programs were not present in the beginning of that summer. The beginnings of militant and nationalist strategies were. Under the surface of cooperation one could see the start of resentment. Why were so many whites running the Movement? Why were "local projects" led by so many "outsiders"? Whose movement was it anyway?

The FST was implicated in all this because we felt that we were part of the Movement. We were in the vanguard of the nonviolent strategy (SNCC once meant non-violence). The theater would say in art what the Movement had been saying in politics. Gandhi and Martin Luther King were right. Masses of people can be moved, and their love can change things. Experience was to prove us wrong, was already proving us wrong as we hammered out the program.

I left Jackson feeling very good. I felt heroic. Here I was, a white Jewish boy whose family lived in South Orange, New

Jersey (they had fled Newark, but I didn't think of it as "flight"), working with "them," helping them, participating myself. I was making "theater meaningful." I was tying aesthetics into politics. I was part of the "Second American Revolution." All that can be very heady. But as I drove back to New Orleans, through the strawberry fields sweet-smelling and hot, I wondered where my commitment really was. Would I give up my professorship? Would I resign from *TDR*? Was all this a lark, or was it something that would change my life?

Obviously, I did not give up my professorship or *TDR*. I defined myself as not-quite-in the FST. I would "do all I could" to help. But I stopped short of commitment. It was not my problem alone. Somehow few of us in the FST ever gave up life styles and adapted new ones to suit the situation. It didn't seem necessary then. Gil and John gave unstintingly of their time. They made the FST their theater. But Gil was never able to relate directly to the people he was performing for and John could never apply the leadership principles he enunciated so eloquently. The theater moved along without defined leadership. It never knew to whom or what it owed its soul. We had some thrilling generalities and some moving performances. But the middle term—the translating and transforming organization between rhetoric and reality—was missing. We never truly linked up.

Hints and scraps—evidence of why we didn't—are strewn over four years of struggle. It is a complicated story. The outcome of the experience is not yet clear. And perhaps the organic way the FST developed (or, if you will, its chaotic development) is precisely what is called for in the Southern situation. To unravel these questions, and to relate the FST's importance, means to continue my rambling account, and let the pieces fall in place.

I went away for the summer of 1964. Gil and John stayed in Jackson to lay the groundwork for the FST. I went to New York, ostensibly to do research for a book on Eugene Ionesco. A book

I was never to complete. My other New York assignment was to begin structuring the FST: help organize a New York committee, draw up incorporation papers, see about fund-raising.

That summer, while I was in New York, the FST truly began. Gil and John were organizing things in Jackson. Chaney, Schwerner, and Goodman were murdered that July. Freedom summer moved into the intolerably hot and muggy (for a Northerner) August that marks the Gulf States. It seemed imperative that the FST begin at once, during the summer, before even the beginnings of its organization were completed. And *In White America* seemed the perfect script. Martin Duberman's collation of documents and scenes from American history, an underground history of the black man in these peculiar states, was appropriate for several reasons. Even ironic. Duberman—a white Jewish professor at Princeton. A play which had a "successful run" (as they say) off Broadway; a text which was heart-rending, sentimental, but certainly not Black Nationalist (precious few scenes and less sympathy was given to the Nationalists). The play matched the temper of Freedom Summer, the time of "black and white together."

Surely, as a historian, Duberman would agree that you cannot judge one epoch by the standards of another or one culture by the ethos of another. Thus I must not knock *In White America*. At the same time, in the perspective of 1968, the play is condescending, patronizing. It is the nearly perfect representation of "liberal sentiment," and it reveals—if we look at it carefully—precisely where that sentiment failed the Freedom Movement. (I should add quickly and approvingly that Duberman's own politics have kept pace with evolving events. I don't think he would compile *In White America* today in the same way as he did in the early sixties. He might even demur from attempting it altogether realizing that he can no more escape his own ethnocentrism than Malcolm X could his.) *In White America* is also a revealing episode of FST history because the

FST was never—and perhaps should never be—an "independent" theater. It is tied to the Freedom Movement and to the fate of black people in America.

So Gil and John jumped in. They put together a cast made up of Freedom Workers, some of whom were actors and musicians; they added a sequence dealing with Chaney, Goodman, and Schwerner; they took advantage of the network of COFO offices (the over-all Freedom network in Mississippi that summer), and toured twelve towns in August. For the first time in memory, black audiences confronted episodes in their own American history. But, as I said, these episodes were slanted toward sentimentality: the oppression that black man has suffered, the guilt this oppression has aroused, the stolidity of non-violence, the hope in the future. *In White America* capsuled this appealing but soft-hearted approach to racism in America, and signified the idealism of the early Freedom Movement. It also represented exactly what the FST was when it started. We *shall* overcome. Love *is* stronger than hate. Moral weapons are superior to military or economic weapons. What astonishment this message must have evoked in the white racists of Mississippi! It is a powerful message, frustrated only by people who will not yield to moral suasion. The early FST was predicated on the premise that white America did not know, and that once it found out, truly found out, the inherent goodness of all human beings would prevail. It takes more than several murders and many assaults to dissuade young people from that opinion. But we were dissuaded.

The first summer ended with elation. Autumn brought a harder reality. I returned to New Orleans, having structured the FST corporation in New York but failing in my major mission of raising funds. Honestly, I did not want to be the organizer for the FST, its fund-raiser, its administrator. I wanted to direct plays. And therefore I was less than efficient in the pursuit of my assigned tasks. I was not South during Freedom Summer and I did not do my work North. I copped out. The contradictions between who I was and who the FST wished me to be were very great. It was during 1963 and 1964 that my editorship of *TDR* had begun to bring me a reputation. I was not saintly enough to trade that in for $35 a week and a theater of amateurs. I rationalized that I could best serve the FST from my Tulane position. Perhaps this was true. But there is no way to fudge my lack of work. I simply was not interested in fund-raising or administration.

The fact is that no one in the FST was interested in those things. We always saw them as compromises, both for the theater and for ourselves. The FST was for the people: its support should spring from the people. If it was a black theater, then why seek so much white money? If we were artists, as we presented ourselves to each other, then why mess around with the dreary work of organization? As with everything else ambivalent about the FST, these attitudes had both good and bad consequences. The theater was never well organized; funding was never efficient, and continues to be catch as catch can. But the theater never lacked vitality, all the way through the ranks. No one ever worked for the FST because it was a job. One had to love the damned thing to put up with it.

In the fall of 1964 we worked toward our first "real tour." The "official opening" of the theater. *In White America* had, of course, already opened the theater; the August tour was successful. But we wanted something more formal to kick it off. The August tour had been squeezed out of Gil and John by events; now they would make their own events. The three of us were producing directors, supposedly full partners in the operation. But they were black and working full time for the FST and I was still who I was. We met and argued many days about what plays we would do. We talked of *Blues for Mister Charlie* and other black plays. We argued whether or not they were "accurate reflections" of the "black experience." I knew nothing of that experience, and I suspect that Gil and John knew less of it (in the South) than they thought. We rejected the

Baldwin play and chose instead Ossie Davis's *Purlie Victorious*. An ambivalent choice. Surely in many ways *Purlie* is a liberating play. But in other ways it, like *In White America,* offers a sentimental path to freedom. We opened it in November and toured it, along with *Waiting for Godot,* through January. (The only Southern production of *Blues* I saw, amazingly enough, was at the New Orleans Parish Prison, performed by inmates before an integrated inmate audience. It was quite a performance. Incisive enough to lead to the dismissal of the prison recreation director.)

Our audience loved *Purlie.* Here was a stereotype of Southern rural life, here was the language of the people. Or was it the language of the people? I am still not certain. Surely the rhythms and words were there. But I suspect that this was Delta Broadway, the *Plaza Suite* of the Mississippi flatlands. Or, perhaps, a black *Tobacco Road.* You see, one of the most urgent and always present FST problems is repertory. Exactly what plays to do. We arrived at a time and in a place when there was nothing available. We had our college educations and we wished, probably unconsciously, to "uplift" the people—to present them with the "best." Thus *Godot.* At the same time we wanted to "speak their language." And there was always the persistent knowledge that "their language" was not "our language." Often, even now, this deep problem is glossed over, and not only by the FST. How to speak to without speaking at, how to communicate without patronizing. What alternatives are there other than insult and demogoguery? Other than ignoring a culture and whipping people up to slaughterhouse wars? This problem was focused in the FST by our discussions about repertory. We tried just about everything. Brecht, Beckett, Davis, O'Casey, Ionesco. We sought black plays by black writers and black plays by white writers. (I remember a puppet morality play written by a white South African in 1927. The author had a black panther eat up hypocritical and oppressive white justice.) But it is just this year that a number of black plays are becoming available, plays written by young writers, the children of the Movement and of Nationalism. I hope the FST does some of these plays. If not, it will remain a theater without a literature.

The first tour was very successful, if you measure success by the number of people attending and their responses. Each performance was followed by a discussion, and people saw in both *Purlie* and *Godot* images of their own lives. The company, eight dedicated but exhausted young people, was, by turns, elated and defeated by the tour. No one knew how grueling the winter tour would be. The Freedom Summer people had mostly gone home. The cold monsoons were upon Mississippi and Louisiana. Harassment was constant and frequently dangerous. A period of reaction against Freedom Summer was setting in, among both the blacks and the whites. Bombing was a regular event, and the white summer college kids had "deserted" the cause. The beginnings of Nationalism as a force in the South were visible everywhere. The people who lived there had to do by themselves what had to be done. Mississippi wasn't, after all, the Newport Folk Festival.

I stayed behind in New Orleans. I drove up to McComb for the *Godot* production there. But already I sensed that my relationship with the theater was tenuous. I was soon to be leaving for Montreal for six weeks at the National Theater School. I had lost contact with most company members. Gil, John, and I saw each other frequently enough, but I was becoming not a partner but an adviser. And someone whose advice was all the more suspect because I hadn't been there. "The Tour" was the FST's Crispin's Day. Wounds—both internal and actual—sustained there were the marks of knowledge and dedication. I was an armchair revolutionary. I taught my classes and offered opinions. In January I resigned as producing director.

Not in bitterness but in recognition that I could not make the leap. Later, of course, I realized that had I been able to make that long leap it would have been superfluous. The FST was correctly moving toward becoming an all-black (or very nearly all-black) theater. I became the chairman of the Board of Directors. My functions did not change much. My house was a meeting place. (I had a big apartment. Murray Levy once called it, contemptuously, a "mansion," which it was not.) When the company was in town, frequently enough someone was staying at my apartment. I ran some classes for the FST in theater theory. And we put together a Board. It was a black professional and white liberal board. Very middle class, very well intentioned, and very ineffectual. It was meant to be ineffectual because neither Gil nor John wanted power to pass from their hands. I agreed. The FST Board, at the beginning, was a service organization dedicated to feeding members of the company, ratifying decisions, suggesting ways to raise money, and donating from their own pockets the necessary $500 lumps needed to keep the theater alive.

But the Board surprised us all. It became stronger. At a certain time in 1965 and 1966 it was the only thing that held the FST together. Several members of the Board have been with it from the beginning, and as the race issue began blowing the FST apart (in the winter of 1965–1966), they mediated between factions, made crucial decisions, appointed new leaders, and helped the theater through its most difficult trauma: the departure of both Gil and John.

John left because he was a conscientious objector and he was assigned alternative service in New York. He had applied to his draft board for work on the FST, but with the typical punishment mentality his board decided that John should work away from his interests. He was assigned, finally, to a children's home and the FST suffered his loss. John had been a major stabilizing factor. His way of slow, sometimes tedious, frequently brilliant analysis and his understanding, compassionate humor had seen us all through many struggles. Don't get me wrong. John is a tough-minded man. But he is also a wise human being, a person who can sense what troubles the person confronting him and a man who knows how to use time to smooth out trouble spots.

On the other hand, John was—perhaps because of his very qualities as a thinker and conciliator—a slovenly administrator. He would spend hours answering a business letter, would answer it with care, not as much for the business matter at hand as for the human being who asked the question. John was always very aware of the particular historical circumstance of the FST and the Movement, he had many friends in the Movement, and he maintained an extensive dialogue. The day-to-day drear of running the FST was not his cup of tea. Had he had a well-trained office staff handling routine matters, he would have been a perfect administrator. But there were few people in the office, too much to do, and too many troubles. Helen Brown (at that time, my wife) was a godsend to the office. She was efficient and thorough, knew how to organize things, and kept the FST office in existence for the better part of the 1965–1966 fall and winter. But she wasn't enough, and her relationship to the FST emotionally was even more tenuous than mine. So John left and what little administrative steam the FST had went with him.

Gil's leaving was more attenuated and related to deeper issues than John's forced leave of absence. John has continued to work for the FST, has put the New York office in top shape, and has been instrumental in FST policy. He plans to return as soon as his service is over. (For some mad bureaucratic reason John's service was extended: some of his "time" was "bad," according to the people who make such decisions.) When Gil left he left for good, and probably for good reasons.

As I have said, the FST began with a somewhat standard liberal program. Among the first companies were James Cromwell and Murray Levy, two white actors of considerable talent. Cromwell directed *Godot,* I directed *Purlie.* The FST was an *integrated* theater—not only in fact, but in intention and ideology. We were a response to the early Freedom Movement, the cultural outgrowth of a tide of sentiment which cried, "Give the Negroes their due!" But most of us hardly understood what these dues were or how deeply racism was written in the American soil. Perhaps the black members of the FST knew, but were keeping quiet. Most probably even they, being young, could not sense the immensity of black American history or the incalculable reservoirs of hatred which flowed beneath the reassuring tides of "love thy enemy." At any rate, by the middle of 1965 the *Autobiography of Malcolm X* was available. This book had a profound impact on the members of the FST. It was something in itself: a clear and forceful statement of Northern black experience, a chronicle of one brilliant man's search for status on his own terms and through his own people. The tones of reconciliation with which Malcolm ended that book were there, but muted. He was assassinated before these tones became dominant. What was most clearly there was the pride, the self-help, the hatred of the white man, and the beautiful dignity of Malcolm.

The *Autobiography* was more than a tide-turning book. It represented the second phase of the Movement. In its first phase, the Movement worked from Southern conferences and drew Northerners South. The fight was at first legal and then in the streets. It was a fight for simple recognition. "Look, man," the early Movement said, "here we are. We live here, too. Move over and give us some room. Some breathing space. Some living space." The strategies of the Southern Movement—litigation, sit-ins, mass marches—were directed against a society that would not even grant the most obvious legislative recognition to the black community. The second phase of the Movement was in the other direction. It originated in the Northern ghettos and flowed South from there. This was not the doctrine of nonviolence and love, but of separation and resistance. The whole flow of the Movement was reversed. There is no tangible difference between segregation and separatism. The difference is intangible. If you're segregated, someone is *making* you stay in your place; if you're separate, you *choose* to band together with your own people. I don't know if either segregation or separatism has much of a productive future in America. They are not systems that I can support. At the same time, integration into the majority means adoption of middle-class values. Worse, it means that the black community will never have much of a say in politics. In America each community must go through its separatist and nationalist phases; and the black community more violently than others because blacks were slaves and then second-class, and they will always be immediately identifiable. Thus, if the causes of separatist sentiment disappear, the race itself will disappear with it. I leave to others more versed in these matters the detailed discussion of them. I wish to point out only that the Movement found a new ideological home in the Northern ghettos, and even Southern leadership adapted Northern ways of approaching problems. The Southern style—most clearly represented by Martin Luther King—fell into disrepute, at least among black intellectuals and rebels (frequently the same people). This switch in strategy came from a changed perspective, brought to the FST by Malcolm's *Autobiography*.

I remember very well talking to Denise Nicholas in New Orleans during the early spring of 1966. "I never knew I was black," she said, "until I read Malcolm." Somehow typically, for the intellectual types that made the FST, experience was not validated until it was authoritatively written out. All around us was black experience, and for the black members of the company life was a largely black experience. But Malcolm had to write his book before we believed it. I suspect that it was not that way with Malcolm himself. He was a man of the streets, a man of talking not writing, of doing not theorizing. But we were of a different kind.

As the Northern ideology came South, it awakened in Gil deep thoughts about the FST's blackness. He was a Northerner and he was more at home in that frame; Malcolm's ideas entered swiftly into his own developing awareness. And within a few months the discussion was no longer should the FST be all-black, but how were we going to make the FST all-black? The decision had repercussions all the way down the line. I was white, some members of the company were white, the majority of the Board were white. A racial tension surfaced at our Board meetings. "I can't talk to you," Gil once shouted at me. "You're white!" The underground issue was out in the open. Several Board members resigned. None in anger, a few in fear, and several in disgust. It was not that we wanted these members to stay. We almost too eagerly accepted their resignations. And we began to add "local black people" to the Board. People who were not ministers or doctors, but community leaders—people close to the ghetto, who lived there and understood the ghetto's values.

And then it was my turn. It is difficult for me to describe dispassionately and objectively my feelings at the time. I was turned-off by the FST. I was tired of racial squabbling. I wanted to be left alone. At the same time I didn't want to be squeezed out. I had invested time and energy in the theater. I thought my position—make the theater black, but not all-black—was a sensible one. I wanted to retain some power in the theater. But because Gil and I were talking about real and personal things—and yet things that were imposed on us—talking became very difficult. I think the majority of the Board supported my position. But in the FST then, as always (and, I really think, correctly), the majority vote of the Board was irrelevant. The people running the theater had to be heard, especially the black people. And they wanted an all-black theater. If it wasn't to be all-black then they would quit and the FST would be all-white, or worse: a black theater recruited and directed by whites. I quit as Board chairman and Gil quit as artistic director. We were both ready to quit anyway. For personal reasons. I was becoming interested in happenings and environmental theater and I thought the FST was necessary but square. Gil wanted to go back North, write, study acting, make music. Other purely personal problems beset members of the company. And in the context of New Orleans and Mississippi, the usual tensions that beset theater groups were magnified. Thus the time had come for a real change in leadership and the end of a series of false withdrawals. For a time Gil was "just a company member," and outside artistic directors were brought in. But this didn't work. The company was too small for one of the founders to vanish in the ranks. It just confused the leadership issue.

My resignation, Gil's resignation, and Tom Dent's appointment as chairman of the Board were effected over a series of discussions led by John, who flew down from New York. Tom was a more active chairman than I had been. He quit his job to devote full time to the FST. He was involved with the company, ran writing workshops, and began the difficult and long-overdue task of building the FST organization. I stayed on the Board and attended meetings and offered my advice. But my truly active days with the FST were over. I had mixed feelings about that. At the same time, I knew that I had not been a very effective leader and that it was impossible and wrong for a white to maintain a leadership position with the theater.

Tom's appointment ended the debate about an all-black theater. Tom issued fewer proclamations than Gil, John, or I had. But his work was solid and perhaps, essentially, more radical than ours had been. Like us he was a writer. But he was not primarily interested in theater—could therefore take a more dispassionate view of it—and, most importantly, he was from New Orleans. Under his leadership the theater has not been all-black. Murray Levy stayed on as an actor and director—though Murray's frequent assertions that he was "going to leave" became a standard joke. Richard Aronson served as general manager for some months. But in more essential ways the FST became a black theater. We sought and did scripts by black writers, including Gil's *Roots.* We put together shows of black music and poetry. Tom built a strong Board and community program. As at the very beginning I became a simple adviser. I remained on the Board, but I no longer ran it. And as Tom gathered together some young people from the community to assist in the productions, I found myself farther and farther from the center of the FST.

I remember a trip I took with Tom and some of the workshop members to Bogalusa. It was fun, and exciting. The Deacons for Defense and Justice gave us an armed escort in and out of town. We played pool. We performed. But the kids in the car with us —I could talk to them less well than to Gil. Gil had been to college, and he was an intellectual. If race separated us, education and class brought us together. But these young writers were out of my range. I was actually, at times, afraid of them—the old, racial fears compounded by class suspicion and the lack of an intellectual vocabulary on their part and a street vocabulary on mine. This vocabulary gap is not one of words, but of concepts—of handling thoughts, images, patterns. It is at the root of the breakdown in communication between large groups of people in this country. And I felt this gap acutely.

Tom is an intellectual. But he is at home in many contexts. Of all the people who have led the FST he is the most versatile. That does not mean that the theater has flourished under his leadership. But without him, the theater would have died in 1966. He began, and continues, to repair old damage and build toward sound programs. He has not been able to solve the basic FST problem: finding and keeping good actors and directors. But he has dealt successfully with the problems next in importance: organization, local support, local workshops, national funding.

As I come close to the end of this story, I can offer no advice about how the FST will get and keep artists. The ideal solution is for the theater to develop its own artists. But to enunciate this once again is to proclaim the old rhetoric without suggesting how to attain the goal. Somehow the Northern strategy has become focused in the North and today the FST seems quaint to many people. The FST is quaint and the South is frightening. The action is in Harlem and Watts, Detroit and Newark. In the

South people are still fighting for recognition, and progress is slow, experience often humiliating. Actors don't want to leave the big cities or suffer segregation when revolution is in the air. Some of the blame can be put at the FST's feet. It has never really developed a strong repertory of black plays. I never heard of black writers like Ben Caldwell, Marvin X, Dorothy Ahmad, and Ed Bullins until Bullins edited a special Black Issue of *TDR*. Why weren't these names mentioned in FST discussions? Why did the FST have Douglas Turner Ward's *Day of Absence* and not produce it? (We thought the play wasn't quite "finished," not really "ready.") How is it that Denise Nicholas is now with the Negro Ensemble Company and Roscoe Orman with the New Lafayette Theater (along with two or three other FST veterans)? Why couldn't we keep these very talented performers with us?

The answer lies in some difficult observations and painful conclusions. No one could translate the FST from rhetoric to reality. Through all the theorizing no strong program of black plays was ever presented; no leader emerged who was both willing and able to take the project in hand and direct it. The FST straddles a lot of fences. We take money from the National Endowment and the Rockefeller Foundation. We participate in Poverty Program projects. And we try to tell people that we are at once (for the black kids in the ghettos) a revolutionary theater (for the black professionals on our Board and living in "good" neighborhoods), a professional theater like the regional theater (for the government), a theater that will help "bring culture" to the "underprivileged," and (for the foundations) an alternative to race war. And for ourselves? I don't know.

I love the FST. It has been an important part of my life. I hope for it in the future. I even have confidence that it will find its own tune to play. This tune will probably be raucous but not essentially revolutionary—the theater may even be a force for eventual reconciliation in the South, if that is possible. Naturally, I remember the theater most clearly from its early years when I was closest to it. But I think that Tom's leadership has essentially set the FST on a proper course. One which leads to a confrontation with blackness and the Southern situation. If I remember the black kids rocking my father's car and my first tentative meeting with John and Gil, I remember as well a simple event in Bogalusa in 1965 during a reprise performance of *In White America.* I was sitting in the hot room where the performance was to take place. The town was still restless from a summer of violence and murder. Cops were cruising the streets. The Deacons were out with sidearms. It was September and sweltering. I was one of very few whites in the audience. Standing near the door was an immense black man. He must have been six-ten and three hundred pounds.

I turned to a young man sitting next to me, pointed at the black giant, and asked, "Who is that?" "I don't know, baby," my informant told me. "But if his name was Boy, I'd call him *Mister* Boy if I was you."

Dignity, in its widest and deepest sense—that is the goal of the FST. In whatever color that comes, it cannot but be a good thing for us all.

Richard Schechner

New Orleans: Blacks, Whites, and the Ninth Ward

The Reverend Milton Upton, a native of Tennessee, has been pastor of the Beecher Memorial Church in New Orleans for the past eight years. He was the first member of the New Orleans black community to get and stay involved with the Free Southern Theater, and is now chairman of our Board of Directors.

New Orleans has not had traditional patterns of racial, residential segregation, as in many other communities. It is a community of Catholic influences. All the priests were white, many black kids attended parochial schools and they didn't get any kind of historical perspective on the role of the black man in America. They didn't get any in the public schools either. So I have to say the black man in New Orleans has been rather sheltered a long time and doesn't really know his history. He needs the kind of thing FST is doing to make him aware that we, black people, have made a significant contribution to the growth, to the culture of this country. I saw a television program a few months ago in preparation of the 250th anniversary celebration of the founding of New Orleans. This entire program, an hour or so in length, showed absolutely nothing of the black man's contribution to the development and growth of New Orleans. In almost any other community this kind of exclusion would have aroused the black community, but it didn't happen here. People viewed it as entertainment and didn't give it a thought.

Of course the best example of the city's consistent disregard-until-it's-too-late attitude was the "Look Up and Live" crisis.

The city expected the white FST Board members to cancel the show to be in complete accord with their request. They found out that this was not the case, and it infuriated the city to no end. This is a commendable thing—well, I don't know if it's commendable or not: you don't commend people for being human and decent, though there may be times when that becomes necessary because of the indecent people.

Then the New Orleans Housing Authority sent a couple of its board members to CBS in New York to see if they could get our section cut out of the program. They got nowhere; it was shown in August 1966 in many cities, but not in New Orleans. The city was very much concerned about its image; it did not want the world to know it had this ghetto down here called the Desire Housing Project. It has miserable human beings living in it, made miserable by conditions of overcrowdedness. There is only one street that goes in and out. Trains block both the entrance and the exit. At that time they had only one swing that was working, one backstop for baseball. So that these were people who were kept out of the city and relegated to this area and forgotten.

They claimed that showing this film would possibly instigate a riot because August 1966 was rather close on the heels of the Watts riot.

Before they went to CBS in New York the manager of the Authority called together twelve white New Orleans clergymen, including the executive secretary of the Federation of Churches and a high official in the Archdiocese of the Roman Catholic Church, the executive secretary of the Baptist group here, the Lutherans and other church officials. Only two of these twelve men had ever *seen* the Desire Housing Project. These men were all white; there were no black clergy involved in this meeting. They were asked to condemn the scheduled program and do whatever they could to prevent it. They said frankly they could not pass judgment on something they had not seen. It did spark their going into the area and taking a look at it. That involved the Inner-City Clergy, Inter-Faith Committee, of which I happen to be a member. As a result of this confrontation with the Housing Authority I invited them to hold our next meeting in the Desire area, in the Lutheran church located at the edge of the Housing Project, so they could get a first-hand look at what actually existed. They did and they refused to condemn the program.

The black community in New Orleans, as I see it, is not willing to take too many risks, is not willing to get involved in too much controversy. Most of the so-called progress we have made here has not been made because of any efforts of our own so much as it has been following the tail of other Southern cities. The support we have tried to get for the theater has been a hit-and-miss kind of thing. Though this is a metropolitan area, too many people have simply never seen legitimate theater; not only the people who live in the ghetto, but many of the middle-income group have not seen theater. In the early days when FST announced that it was going to perform this and that, people came out not really knowing what to expect, except fun and entertainment. They didn't expect serious reflection and introspection.

The FST was a shocker, and it still is a shocker to people. And then perhaps people felt, "Well, it's free, they get their money from someplace else, they don't need my money anyway." So people didn't give too much. We tried to have a party here sponsored by the Friends of FST. We got very little money. One way I can think of to get money from middle-class New Orleans black people is to hand them something on a silver platter, give them something special, tell them they are something special, treat them special, and they will respond. Otherwise, they couldn't care less what happens. They would much rather give their money to the opera or to the repertory theater, or invest it in the Mardi Gras Ball.

If we had a building that was located in what is considered the "right" location, not where we are now, down in that filthy Ninth Ward, that slum area, that ghetto area, that poor area down there, but in the central city with bright lights and so forth, with some semblance of Broadway, then middle-class blacks would come see the plays. But they don't want to come into our building, they don't want to come into our area, they complain that they are afraid of this and that.

I mentioned the fact that the white clergymen had not been into the area. I don't want to leave this out: so many, many, many of the black middle-class community or middle-income community have not been in that area either. Those who go into the area are those who work there, like schoolteachers and so forth. It just doesn't exist as far as the others are concerned. If the theater could ever draw them in, could ever get support in any way, it would really be a milestone; it would be a landmark in the history of the city of New Orleans.

Because FST is an idea and an ideal. It's a challenge. It works because of the people. FST is flexible, FST is a group of people designed to meet the need and who can change horses in middle stream, so to speak. We aren't dealing with theater in the Broadway or traditional sense. We are dealing with people and with ideas peculiar to our people and their conditions. We are seeking to discover, to create, and to develop talent. How many theaters have this kind of workshop program where anybody can come in and become involved and have the free run to develop themselves as fully as their potential will let them?

FST is quite definitely related to the way we think of ourselves as black people. Nowhere in New Orleans in the public schools, private schools, and universities is there being done the type of thing that we are doing.

Rev. Milton Upton

A Look Ahead

I came to New Orleans from New York on April 1, 1965. New Orleans was the town of my birth and early adolescence but I had not lived there since I went away to school in the early 1950s. I was an aspiring writer, had many writer friends in New York, none in New Orleans. I had no intention of staying in New Orleans, but was trying to arrange for a job in New York. I had known about the Free Southern Theater, had known Doris Derby in New York before she went South, and had met John O'Neal. Though I did not see the New School performances I had read the *Village Voice* reviews and was impressed.

Since nothing happens culturally in New Orleans for black people (whites either), I looked up the Free Southern Theater immediately. At about the same time, I discovered that the FST was scheduled to perform Brecht's *Carrar* at Dillard University. This was the first FST performance I saw and it left an indelible impression on me.

A group of white and black youths rode into that bastion of colored respectability, Dillard, in blue jeans and tee shirts in trucks like a traveling circus, to set up lights and stage. The play was not impressive in itself. The audience was small. The production was not smooth or polished. They were trying to hit the audience with a very direct statement and I was swept away. There was something in the energy, the seriousness, the lack of arty phoniness, and yes, a kind of idealism, that made me believe instantly that the project had both social and artistic value.

After the show, all the actors lined up on the stage, sitting with their legs hanging (destruction of the stage illusion), to discuss the play with the audience. Roscoe Orman had done a beautiful son; his eyes were intense with interest, listening for reaction. He was just down from New York. Richard Schechner (the first time I had seen him) made a long, often brilliant comment on the failure and problems of the play as an FST vehicle. While the discussion developed, the stage props came down, everyone joining in, like a joyful ritual. The fact that it was integrated, that it had that aura of disrespect for tradition and artiness, made it impressive. A hell of a lot of challenge to the unconscious assumptions of an audience became possible. All this in the wake of considerable local publicity about harassing arrests of an integrated group from the company a week or so earlier in the French Quarter. The FST was new, exciting, and dangerous. I wanted to be part of it—there was really nothing else for me in New Orleans—and I began hanging around every day, doing what I could.

As I became more involved with the FST I discovered that the organization was beset with administrative and artistic contradictions. There were too many people who had no clear idea of what they should be doing. There was no administrative clarity; the leaders, John O'Neal, Gil Moses, and Cordier were simply overwhelmed, particularly O'Neal, who had the basic responsibility of making some sense out of things.

There were deeper problems. Most revolving around race. By the middle of the summer there were almost twice as many whites as blacks in the company. Almost all of the white kids had never been in the South before, knew nothing of black people. The situation paralleled that of SNCC and COFO in 1964 and 1965. Communication between blacks and whites in the theater was difficult, becoming increasingly more difficult. Was it a black theater, regional theater, "integrated" theater, or what? With the extreme cleavage of races in the South, it was a fact that the FST was playing to black audiences only. The only whites who ever came were working in the Movement. The FST was in a black community and FST people lived in black communities on tour. If the whites in the company had no knowledge of or experience with black people, how could they possibly play a dominant or significant role in shaping a theater which was designed to play to these people? Those of us who were black began to express, to each other, the feeling that the FST, though a good idea, had the quality of grafted art. *In White America* was not really apropos or contemporary enough; neither was Brecht. Something else was needed, and the whites couldn't help shape that, because they didn't know *what* was needed, no matter how much technical theater training they brought South.

Now I feel what we are struggling toward, particularly in our workshop program, has to do with planting seeds so that the theater can grow in the garden of black cultural consciousness. Any theater which attempts to grow, to live by itself, justifying its own artistic ideals but failing to relate to the people around it, to the community, is grafted theater. It is bringing culture to the masses. We have all realized by now that not only can this not be done, but the black masses have no need of such benevolence. Blacks already have the richest, most viable, most complex and rewarding culture in this potpourri of America. The battle is not one of bringing culture to black people, but of us learning to value, and affirm, the culture we already have—and, as far as the performing company is concerned, to adapt that culture, that strength, to the stage.

What are these cultural strengths? They are those aspects and institutions of black culture which have not been totally absorbed by mass white American culture: our church, our music, our dance, our communal forms of protest against racial injustice. Otis Redding, James Brown, the black Baptist Church, the Movement demonstrations, are theater. We don't call them theater, but they are. They have all the requisites of theater: message, actors, ritual, audience, stage, common assumptions between audience and performer. They have entertainment. If any community loves theater, has always had a theater, it is the black community in America. Why shouldn't a black *Theater* move right in and capitalize on these forms, these rituals of theater that already exist? This is the only way to conceive of the FST; this is the way our theater will succeed.

To bring Broadway, off-Broadway, even radical white theater as it exists today in America, to the black community is most irrelevant. It is a statement of negation, if taken too seriously. It means, it is saying to this community which already has its own thing, refined past the point where whites in America can even understand its subtleties, it is saying, "What you have ain't shit. If you want to be 'cultured' you got to dig *Godot*." Well, I say goodbye *Godot,* we'll stick with Otis. We'll expand, and develop, from that. And the hell with what the white critics say or expect. It's as simple as that.

Thomas C. Dent